Clutter to Clarity

A Simple Guide to Decluttering Your Life,
Reaching Your Goals & Creating Breakthroughs

ANGEL RICHARDS

HELPING OTHERS TRANSFORM, LLC

Copyright ©2017 by Angel Richards

Published by Helping Others Transform, LLC Tampa, FL

All rights reserved. No part of this book may be reproduced or transmitted in any form or by any means, electronic or mechanical, including photographing, recording or by any information storage retrieval system without written permission from the author, except for the inclusion of brief quotations in a review.

Cover Design & Book Design: Mad House Design Inc
Photograpger: Shutter Nduljence
Editor: Kingdom Helper

ISBN 978-0-692-89543-6

THIS BOOK IS DEDICATED TO ALL THE WOMEN AND MEN WHO HAVE JOINED ME ON THIS CLUTTER FREE JOURNEY. HERE'S TO MORE PEACE, HAPPINESS, AND SUCCESS.

TO MY CHILDREN QUAMARIUS, TANYLA, EVA AND AVA... YOU ARE MY MOTIVATION, MY INSPIRATION AND MY REASON WHY. I AM HONORED TO BE YOUR MOM. YOU MAKE ME PROUD. LOVE YOU.

Contents

Welcome Letter 5

Introduction: My Journey From Clutter to Clarity 6

SESSION 1. Declutter Your MIND 15

SESSION 2. Declutter Your HEART 23

SESSION 3. Declutter Your SPIRIT 32

SESSION 4. Declutter Your BODY 41

SESSION 5. Declutter Your RELATIONSHIPS 49

SESSION 6. Declutter Your CONVERSATIONS 57

SESSION 7. Declutter Your FINANCES 64

SESSION 8. Declutter Your ENVIRONMENT 73

SESSION 9. Declutter Your HABITS 80

SESSION 10. Clarify Your VISION 90

SESSION 11. Clarify Your PURPOSE 98

SESSION 12. Clarify Your DREAMS 106

SESSION 13. Clarify Your GOALS 111

SESSION 14. Wrap Up 121

Hey love,

I'm so excited and grateful that you said YES to starting your #clutterfree journey!

I wrote this book to help reveal the importance of eliminating clutter from all areas of your life so you can have the CLARITY, CONFIDENCE & COURAGE needed to experience more love, happiness, peace, success, freedom and all of your hearts desires.

Throughout these pages, you will find insight and inspiration for the many issues we face in life. You will also answer many of the same coaching questions I ask my private clients that have helped them gain a deeper level of self-awareness, acknowledge their desires and plan their next steps to take action towards reaching their goals and living thier dreams.

I believe that everything you want is on the other side of the clutter, confusion and chaos you are tolerating so get ready to clear the clutter, GET OUT OF YOUR OWN WAY and create your biggest breakthrough ever.

Prepare to shift your mindset, shake up your belief system and shoot for SUCCESS & SATISFACTION in all areas of your life - because you CAN have it all when you're willing to do the work. There are blessings and breakthroughs with your name on them. So let's unblock them now!

Because its your time!

*XO
Angel*

My Journey from Clutter to Clarity

At the age of 29, I had a nervous breakdown. And it felt like a mid-life crisis.

It wasn't the first time, but it was definitely the last. It happened partly because I was obsessing about turning 30 and not being where I wanted to be in life but also because I had just spent the past year and a half stressed, struggling and settling for less, and it finally got to me.

I was overweight, broke, lonely, angry, insecure and depressed. I had not planned on being a single mom of four who hated her life. Who plans for that? Nobody. Even though I didn't plan for it - I created it. So I was the only one responsible for changing it.

I AM THE SOLUTION.

Many contributing factors led to this moment. I was violated as a young girl by multiple men. Those events left me with so much fear, anger, and hatred. I didn't know how to handle all those strong emotions, so I started to rebel.

Losing my innocence almost made me lose my mind yet nobody seemed to notice. I was seen as just a young girl who was going through changes; a product of my environment. I felt invisible, alone and misunderstood. My cries for help were ignored, so I started to ignore my own pain.

As a result of the violations, I lost trust in all men. I thought they all were perverted, pedophiles, liars, cheaters and couldn't be trusted. I became paranoid and suspicious of them all. And because of what I was experiencing with some of the women in my life around that time, I lost hope in them too. I thought they were all self-centered, back-stabbing, fake and could not be trusted. Unfortunately, this became the cracked foundation on which I tried to build my future relationships... EPIC FAIL! As I came of age, I started to use my beauty and body as a weapon to make men feel my pain. I wanted their attention. I wanted them to fall in love. I wanted them to get jealous. I wanted them to need me so that I could break their hearts like others had done mine. I had a false sense of strength and power that eventually backfired, leaving me even more broken.

Instead of feeling powerful and in control I felt weak, lost, used and taken for granted, which led to my bouts of low self-esteem and self-hatred. But I was stuck. Or so I thought.

WE ARE NEVER STUCK, WE JUST AREN'T MOVING.

All those games I was playing eventually caught up with me. I found myself in abusive relationships and creating a reputation that made even me uncomfortable. I was acting tough as though I could handle all the lies, cheating and embarrassment but I really couldn't. I DID CARE. I did want love. I did want better. But I didn't quite know how to get it. So I failed miserably at my own game.

I soon became a teen mom at 15 years old. The judgment and criticism became unbearable. I was smarter than this, better than this. Why me? I thought everybody else was running the streets; I was just a follower. Why was I the one stuck now? Why was I being punished? My days were filled with depression because I just couldn't believe I was going to be a teen mom and I knew this would set my family back- things were already tight.

I pressed forward and managed to make it through high school with honors. It was hard and I wanted to quit most days but I couldn't. I now had a son who depended on me. I wanted to be a good example for him and to be able to say to him one day, "You were my motivation. Look how far you helped me come." That thought gave me hope and one day those would be the very words I spoke to my son.

But before that moment, there were many more unpleasant ones.

I guess I didn't learn my lesson because at 19 years old I was pregnant again. The struggle was real. But, this time I was living on my own. I had more responsibilities. I had my own apartment in the housing projects and started dating hustlers just to get extra help with my kids. I wasn't the type to ask for things, but with my charm, I got everything I wanted and needed. Their fathers weren't in the picture, so I was doing what I thought I had to do to make it. But all that help came with a cost. A price I didn't want to pay. I did a lot behind those closed doors and shed a lot of tears, but to everyone on the outside looking in - I was smart, strong and doing my thing. I let them believe that, but I knew the truth- I was making dumb decisions, acting weak and depended on men to get by.

LIFE IS ONLY AS HARD AS WE MAKE IT.

I went through a lot of hurt and pain for the next few years, but eventually, things started to turn around. I qualified for Section 8 (housing assistance) which allowed me to move to a nicer community. My kids could finally play outside without being exposed to drug deals and fights. I was finishing up with my bachelor's degree in education and would have an actual career soon. I was very excited to have an income that would help me get to my next level. I was attending church regularly and felt closer to God. I was meeting nice people and started to realize that not everyone was bad or out to get me. I was working out at the YMCA 5 days a week getting my body back in shape. The gym became my healthy way of blowing off steam, and it felt good. My bank account was growing, and so was my confidence. I even went on to become a homeowner at age 25. I had beat the odds. I was doing what nobody thought I would, not even myself. I was in a good place, and there was no turning back.

THERE IS A SEASON FOR EVERYTHING.

Although I had learned how to create success, I did not know how to keep it. I worked hard to get to a good place for myself and my children but things took a turn for the worse. I thought I would never recover.

Although my money was right, my body was tight, and my relationship with God was evolving... I still sucked at relationships. Bad. I dated all the wrong men, for all the wrong reasons for way too long. I had upgraded from disrespectful drug dealers to dysfunctional professionals and thought I was doing better.

On the outside, they appeared to have it together, but on the inside, they were just as broken as I was. Despite all the good I had going for me, my mindset had not caught up yet. There was still a lot of clutter in my life that was lingering and spilling over into other areas. But one thing I had perfected at this point was walking away. Somehow I was this intelligent, accomplished educator with public success being awarded teacher of the year yet suffering in silence in my own home at the hands of an abusive man. It started off mental, verbal and emotional, but eventually became physical.

All the fighting, arguing and abuse was wearing me down. I was tired of calling the cops, tired of going to court, tired of fighting this battle. Like many women, I had become abusive as a way to defend and protect myself. But no matter how tough I tried to be, I was still a woman. A woman who was hurting and needed a way out.

My confidence was gone. My self-esteem was gone. My money was gone. My happiness was gone. My dreams were dead and honestly... I wanted to join them. My depression was back and had taken on a whole new identity. I was suicidal, and I felt extremely lost and helpless. It was a feeling I have never felt before. It was so real. So scary. And that feeling lingered for years to come.

I soon became a single mom of four after having a set of twin girls. I was trying to figure out how I had gotten into such a deep, dark place - a place where I had worked so hard to get out. No matter how much I cried or how hard I prayed- I had no answers. I was lonely, scared and desperate. Then one night I found myself sitting in my bathroom, in the corner, crying my eyes out, screaming at the top of my lungs...

WHY ME?

WHY GOD?

WHAT DID I DO?

I CAN'T DO THIS.

I CAN'T TAKE IT ANYMORE.

And at that moment - God spoke.

IT'S NOT OVER.

At that moment a calm started to take over my body. I had never heard the voice of God before. We weren't all that close anymore. I was full of guilt and shame and confusion, so I had been avoiding Him. But like most people, I called on Him in my most desperate hour, and He answered my call.

I immediately was led to the mirror where I saw myself - eyes red, mascara smeared, mouth trembling, body shaking. I was exhausted. I almost didn't recognize myself.

In just a year I went from reaching my goals and up leveling my life to everything falling apart. I had lost myself and everything else. I felt pitiful and pathetic. I thought... this must be rock bottom because it can't get any worse than this. I looked at myself in the mirror as the tears poured down and I started to speak life into myself and over my situation. That was something I had heard at church but never really tried...

I LOVE YOU.

I AM SORRY.

YOU ARE GOING TO BE ALRIGHT.

YOU DESERVE BETTER.

YOU CAN DO THIS.

YOU ARE GOING TO MAKE IT.

And I repeated those words over and over.

I LOVE YOU. I AM SORRY. YOU ARE GOING TO BE ALRIGHT. YOU DESERVE BETTER. YOU CAN DO THIS. YOU ARE GOING TO MAKE IT.

This time my cry was different. This time my cry had power. Looking back at that moment, I was shifting from breakdown to breakthrough in such a mighty way, and I didn't even know it.

I WAS SHIFTING FROM CLUTTER TO CLARITY.

Shifting, healing and forgiving myself for allowing things to get this bad. It took me some time to truly forgive the people in my life and those who were gone, to heal from my past, to see my worth, to love myself. But I did it. And I did it- one prayer at a time, one decision at a time and one day at a time.

I realized that it was the choices I was making that were recreating this scenario. It was my thoughts, words, habits, friends and environment that needed to change so that I could change. Many of my friends were struggling like me. Stuck in abusive relationships, sleeping around, having babies, wasting money and not taking care of themselves. We were comfortably uncomfortable. But at some point you have to wake up, take responsibility for what you're doing and what you're tolerating and do something different.

NEVER SETTLE FOR LESS THAN YOU DESERVE.

I realized that not only was I suffering but my children were too. They had suffered with me, but I didn't even see it because I was so selfish. I was only worried about myself, my pain, my life. I wanted my relationship to work so bad that I had unconsciously put a man before my children.

I knew better than that, but that's what I was doing. I loved my children, and they knew it. But I was so caught up in what I wanted that I was jeopardizing what they needed - a mom who was happy, whole and complete. They already were without their fathers... they didn't need to lose their mother too.

YOUR KIDS ARE ALWAYS LOOKING, LISTENING AND LEARNING.

By the time I turned 30 my life was being restored. I was getting healthy - physically, mentally, emotionally, spiritually and financially. God was restoring everything I had lost because He had plans for my life. There was still purpose on the inside of me and as he said, IT WASN'T OVER. I thought that meant I wasn't supposed to commit suicide but what He meant was my work wasn't done.

I spent the next two years being intentionally single while I picked up the pieces. It was my way of detoxing my life. My rehab time. It was the best decision I could have ever made. It was hard because as independent as I thought I was, I was very dependent on people's opinions, approval, and company. It gave me time to heal, to rebuild and to go after my dreams again. But this time without carrying all that clutter. My life significantly improved and I felt blessed like never before. Things weren't perfect because I still caught hell from time to time. But with God not just on my side but on the inside... I can conquer the clutter and create breakthroughs every time.

GOD HAS A PLAN.

I would continue on to be an extraordinary classroom teacher helping students learn to read and write. I did so for 13 awesome years. Little did I know I would soon become a full-time life coach, teaching women how to rewrite their own life stories. Teaching them how to use the power of clarity, confidence, and courage to reach their goals and live their dreams. Helping them to declutter their lives and create their own breakthroughs to become unstoppable.

Life wasn't perfect after my breakthrough. I still struggled with my old ways of thinking and old habits. I had a few more failed relationships. I even got married and divorced in less than a year. Crazy! But this time around it was different.

I was strong, confident, and in control of my decisions and my life. Regardless of who came or went... I was still standing. No matter what- worked out or fell through... I was still going. I was committed to living a clutter-free life, and nothing was going to stop me!

MY PEACE, HAPPINESS, AND SUCCESS BECAME NON-NEGOTIABLE.

I hope this book encourages and empowers you to start and stay on your clutter free journey so that you can truly experience God's goodness in all areas of your life. It's a decision that changed my life and one that I know will change yours too.

Are you ready to shift from clutter to clarity?

Of course you are!

Let's make it happen!

Happiness is a choice!

Session One Declutter Your Mind

Mental clarity is key to reaching your goals and living your dreams. It's the key to more peace, happiness, and success. It's the key to living the "good" life we all want. But when your mind is filled with negativity, confusion, and chaos, it weakens your ability to make good decisions, overcome challenges and bounce back quickly.

Did you know that your thoughts become feelings, your feelings become words, your words become actions, your actions become habits, and your habits will determine your destination? Everything that you're thinking, speaking and doing is all contributing and creating the life you're living right now. This is why having mental clarity is important. You are always attracting and creating your next experience... consciously or unconsciously, so why not make it a good one?

You hear a lot of people talking these days about having the right mindset. A success mindset, a millionaire mindset, a Christian mindset, etc. By definition, your mindset is an established set of attitudes. As you know, your attitude is basically how you feel about something or someone. Having the right mindset is having the right attitude but that can only happen if you're having the right thoughts. Thoughts lead to how you feel. Thus your feelings create your attitude, and that is where your mind will be set... set on whatever you are constantly thinking about.

As a teenager my mind was consumed with the pain that I felt from being violated, watching women I loved being abused, witnessing the struggles of my family, and so many other things I shouldn't have had to worry about at that young age. Little did I know, it was turning me into an angry, bitter, depressed woman that would experience the same vicious cycle I had once feared. It was hard to watch and even harder to go through. They say what doesn't kill you makes you stronger. I know that now. But I didn't get my strength until I stopped mentally rehearsing and reliving my past (and you won't either until you choose to let it go).

I also remember in my early 20s suffering from a severe lack mindset. On top of all the fear, doubts and hatred, I became obsessed with what I didn't have. I didn't have a nice home, a nice car, or a good man. I didn't have money, and I didn't have a lot of help. Day in and day out my thoughts revolved around what I was lacking. Every time I thought about where my life was, I felt like crap. I complained all the time and did things that didn't make my situation any better- like spending the little money I did have on stupid things or entertaining guys who clearly were not good for me. It was a vicious cycle of lack and limits. But instead of focusing on the solution, I was fixated on the problem, which solved nothing.

If you are consumed with the challenges of your life, then you know that obsessing over them doesn't change them. But it changes you... for the worse. So I want you to get a grip. Nip it now. You have to shift your thinking from negative to positive, hopeless to hopeful, helpless to unstoppable. Much of what's cluttering your mind are things that you cannot change or have no control over so let's put things into perspective- do what you can and let God deal with the rest.

I know, easier than done. But here's the thing- it's doable. You are smarter than you think and stronger than you feel. You can move past what's haunting, hurting and hindering you. It took me a while to mentally move on but I did it and so can you.

I know this to be true because I spent so many years being negative, pessimistic: a true Debbie Downer. Around 2010, I came across some next level people while training with a network marketing company. I was so inspired by the positivity of the people around me. I had no clue what I was doing. I was a classroom teacher trying to collect some extra coins, but I was open to the opportunity. I had never done anything like it before, but I said yes because I saw the possibilities. Those possibilities seemed unlimited. I was exposed to high-energy personal development training, transformative coaching and live events that really showed me a whole other way of thinking, being and living that

I had not experienced. They were all super motivated and driven and focused on their goals and living their dreams. They had big plans for the future and seemed fearless.

Honestly, I didn't really dream anymore, and my goals were simple- pay my bills, raise these kids and hopefully, one day get married. I had my career, so that's pretty much all I thought I wanted and needed. Let me tell you something: once your mind is exposed, expanded and elevated- it never returns to its original state. I was like a new person, and the old ways of living got old real quick.

NOTHING CHANGES IF NOTHING CHANGES.

After spending a lot of time around this new group of people, my mindset started to shift. I was on fire.

I broke up with my cheating boyfriend, loss weight and started making money in my side hustle. I actually started to realize that who I was deep down inside was enough and that I didn't have to pretend to be someone I wasn't to fit in, which never really worked anyway. I could be fun and goofy, but I could also be studious and ambitious. I could listen to all types of music, not just hip-hop and R&B. I could go to clubs that weren't predominantly black, and I could embrace my Hispanic side without feeling shame. I could go to a church with a white pastor and not feel like a sellout.

I quickly realized that successful people embrace who they are, live unapologetically and go after their goals, no matter what. They don't focus on lack or limits or lies. They live their lives on their terms, and I was ready to do the same.

As I started to shift my mind from clutter to clarity my feelings started to follow. Little by little the insecurities and feelings of inadequacy started to leave. I started to develop a self-love and self-confidence that was unshakable, unbreakable and unstoppable. I felt good about myself and the direction I was going. I had goals, plans, and support.

This was the time when I was introduced to life coaching. I knew that one day I wanted to do for women what my life coach was doing for me.

Although I was transforming and things were changing for me, when I would go back home around my friends and family, I was still somewhat of an outcast. I was seen that way even more than ever because the joy and positivity were seen as fake and phony. They didn't think the Angel they knew could change. But in my heart, I knew I was on the right track and wasn't looking back. I remember saying, "I'm headed to the top. Y'all coming?"

CHANGE YOUR CIRCLE, CHANGE YOUR LIFE.

Now don't get me wrong, I wasn't raised terribly, and I had a few decent friends. I just didn't grow up around a lot of positive, motivated, solution driven people. Most of the people I was surrounded by worked hard, complained a lot and was barely making it. So by default, I worked hard, complained a lot and was barely making it. That was until I realized that that wasn't the only way to live. There was another way. A more clear, confident and courageous way. The more I hung out with my new friends, network and mentors, my passions, purpose, and path became more clear. I started to think differently, talk differently, act differently and live differently. As a result, my life hasn't been the same.

Maybe your mind is stuck in the past, on the pain or your problems but I want you to know that it doesn't have to be. You can start to declutter your mind, let go of the negativity and move on if you make a decision to. The decision will happen in your mind, but the choice will only manifest through action. And that is what this book is all about: YOU taking action.

That's just my story of how I started to clear my mental clutter. You will have your story too. And I can't wait to hear all about it!

I want to expose you to a different way of thinking just as they had done for me. I want to specifically help you develop a clutter-free mindset that has made it possible for myself, my clients and my clutter free community to enjoy our lives to the fullest. It all possible when you declutter your life.

Through the remainder of this book, I will be asking you a lot of questions. Questions that will help bring clarity to your current situation as well as the possibilities that lie ahead. Answer them openly and honestly so that you can transform your life and experience your breakthrough now.

Moment of Clarity

What are the top 3 thoughts consuming and cluttering your mind right now?

In what ways do these thoughts have "power" over you? Describe the influence and impact they have on your life right now. How are they making you act and react to people and situations?

How will your life be different once the mental clutter is removed? The negativity, fears, doubts, and insecurities? Think about the changes you really want to see.

What actions are you willing to take NOW to remove these thoughts that are creating mental clutter? List out all the things you know you can do to release the racket in your mind.

HIDDEN SOURCES OF MENTAL CLUTTER

Be selective on social media. Although it can be fun to scroll and see what's happening with your friends, family, celebrities and even strangers, it often becomes the source of comparison, envy, and insecurity. Sometimes the personal details that you share can open you up to unsolicited opinions, criticism, and drama.

Be mindful of what you watch. Sometimes what you watch on television or read in the magazines, newspapers, and blogs further perpetuates the negativity in your life and relationships. It can leave you fearful, paranoid, anxious and even depressed.

Guard your ears. What and who you listen to on a daily basis can have a great impact on what you think and how you act. Indulging in gossip, excessive venting and non-stop complaining is contagious and toxic. Be it the radio, YouTube or real life conversations with your crew, it's all seeping into your spirit.

Your freedom is in your forgiveness!

Session Two Declutter Your Heart

It's time to release your pain and let go of your past so you can access all the love and happiness that is waiting for you. We all have feelings. Even the toughest of us. Women especially are emotional creatures by nature. However when disappointment, devastation, and depression invade our hearts, we can take things too far and for too long.

IT'S OK NOT TO BE OK.

It's just not ok to stay stuck wallowing in negativity, bitterness, and resentment. You have to forgive yourself for what you may have done or allowed to be done to you. You have to forgive others for their words and actions that hurt and betrayed you. Forgiveness isn't so much about the other person as it is about you. When we hold grudges and record of what others have done to hurt us, we continue to hurt ourselves. It is no longer what they said or did that is causing the pain in this very moment, it's your refusing to let it go that has you remembering, rehearsing and reliving it.

I HEAR IT ALL THE TIME: "I'LL FORGIVE, BUT I WON'T FORGET."

I get it. I've even said it. But here's what I know to be true: You are making a conscious decision to keep remembering the offense. And with those thoughts come feelings. This is why choosing to remember things from your past and bringing up what happened every chance you get holds YOU hostage. Trust me; they aren't worried about it anymore. Neither should you. People will drop bombs and move on about their business like an explosion didn't just happen while you stay lying there wounded. So you have a choice: stay down and depressed or get up and move on. Of course you never really forget, and I definitely don't recommend you acting as if things never happened by suppressing your feelings. What I do recommend is that you be less committed to holding on and more committed to moving on.

Now, this may be the first of many times during your clutter free journey that you roll your eyes at me. It's ok. I told you I was going to help you develop a clutter-free mindset. Well here is one of the biggest shifts you're going to have to make: You are going to have to make a non-negotiable decision to let stuff go. ALL OF IT. Often, the main reason we don't want to let it go is that we somehow think it means the person who hurt us gets a pass. That what they did was ok or that they don't have to be held accountable for their actions. Not true. It was not ok. They don't get a pass. God will deal with them. In the meantime, you still have a life to live and shouldn't be ok living it under the power and control of someone else (especially someone who's no longer around). That is what happens when your mindset is set in the past so are your emotions.

It's time to let go so that you can move on with your life free from the emotional baggage that's been weighing you down for days, weeks, months, maybe years. You must let it go if you want peace, happiness, and success. Emotional clutter is the culprit of fear, doubt, and insecurities- especially in relationships and on the job. It becomes our defense mechanism in that we use it to build up a wall to protect ourselves. But unfortunately, that wall not only keeps out the potential pain, it actually stops love from flowing to you and through you. I know that's not what you intended to happen, but that is what you're doing when you hold on to emotional clutter.

I remember not being able to trust any man around my children. I was overly protective and paranoid. I would always feel like they were too close, too nice, or too helpful. I didn't want to be this way but my heart was still hurting from what was done to me as a child, and I was fearful it would happen to my children. Even words like, "Your kids look just like you." would bother me. I would obsess, if he's attracted to me and they look just like me, maybe he is looking at them sexually too. A lot of the things I would say or the way I would act when we did family things would make guys feel uncomfortable and once my boyfriend called me out on it. I was shocked. It was such a sensitive topic; I didn't think anyone would question me about it. I thought they would understand. But sometimes it's hard for people who have never walked in your shoes to get it. More importantly, even if they do get it, they shouldn't be paying for it. He was upset, offended and sick of my suspicions. I defended myself and felt valid in my actions. But the more I explained why I was the way I was, the more I realized I was in bondage and had to break the chains that were going to cause me to ruin potentially good relationships. As a matter of fact, I know I did. I don't have regrets, but I won't make those same mistakes again.

I'm not sure what your hang-ups are, but we all have them. It could have stemmed from childhood, or all started when you were out on your own. Either way, you can't continue to allow the past to haunt you. And get this: by the past, that includes yesterday. You cannot change what happened yesterday so no need to bring it into today.

I know it's easier said than done. Again, I never said any of this would be easy. However, it can and must be done if you want to enjoy life. Period. I've had to go through it myself multiple times. And each time you let go, you grow. What's so awesome about this shift from clutter to clarity is I was able to forgive the men who violated me as a young girl. I was able to forgive my abusive exes. I was able to forgive my children's absent fathers, and I was able to forgive myself for tolerating and settling for less for so many years. Do I deal with these people today? Not really. Do I deal with the pain they caused? Not anymore. God revealed to me that I was stronger than my strongholds... so I set myself free. Now it's your turn to release your pain and your past on purpose.

YOU MUST DEAL IF YOU WANT TO HEAL.

It may be tempting to not deal with your heart issues, but you have to if you want to heal. Before I decided to deal with my daddy issues and all other kinds of issues, I was constantly finding myself in the same types of relationships.

The guy who is very nice but doesn't have a pot to piss in...
The guy who has a pot to piss in but it was at his baby momma's house...
The guy who had all the potential in the world but no passion...
The guy who thought because I am a single mom of 4 he was doing me a favor...
The guy who wanted a strong woman but was determined to break me down...
The guy who was great in bed but not at anything else...
The guy who didn't know how to love because nobody taught him...
The guy who didn't want me but didn't want anyone else to have me...
The guy who wanted to be a leader but was controlling and abusive...
The guy who wanted a trophy wife but didn't want to earn the trophy
The guy who had no job, no car, no plan but a lot of love...
The guy who wanted to be a power couple but turned it into a power struggle...

I could keep going. To say the least, I have experienced a lot of failed relationships, and this is why I am so passionate about helping you declutter your heart because I know this was all a manifestation of my mess that I didn't address.

YOU DATE AT THE LEVEL OF YOUR CONFIDENCE.

I had so many insecurities, fears, and doubts about relationships and marriage that I consistently settled for less. I overlooked the red flags because I thought love conquers all, so I can just love them to life. Since then, I have learned that love conquers a lot, but love isn't enough. You also need trust, loyalty, respect, patience, compassion, provision... there are qualities and traits that one must possess to have a healthy, lasting relationship or marriage. Because some days you won't like your mate or may even feel like you're "falling out of love"...then what?

HURT PEOPLE, HURT PEOPLE.

Clearing out the clutter in your heart will help you think more clearly, make better decisions and give you the courage to walk away from what you know is not good for you. Emotional clutter can cloud your judgment and even cause you to become desperate for love, attention, and affection. That's a dangerous place to be. And having a clutter free heart doesn't mean it will never get broken. It doesn't make you immune to disappointment either. It just means that it won't be your past experiences contributing and creating confusion and chaos with friends, family, on the job or with your mate. Decluttering your heart allows you to experience emotional healing. You can then go into the relationship whole and complete, willing to give love and ready to receive it.

Moment of Clarity

What are the top 3 things cluttering your heart right now?

In what ways have these things changed the way you feel about yourself, others, and your life?

Are you still holding on to anger and unforgiveness towards yourself or others? Why?

How will you become a different person once your heart is healed and set free?

What actions can you take and are you willing to take NOW to remove these feelings that are cluttering your heart and limiting your ability to live and love freely?

Start Healing Your Heart

Discover the areas of your life where you need emotional healing. The clutter could be coming from a bad break up, getting let go from a job, losing a loved one, dealing with financial strain, or sickness. You must take the time to reflect and figure out what you need to be healed from.

Discuss your feelings with the person who has hurt you or someone you can trust. Sometimes it's best not to talk things out with the person who contributed to the emotional clutter. I believe that in some cases- no closure is a form of closure. Not everyone is mature enough to admit their faults and apologize for their wrong doings so discussing it with them may only make matters worse. But that doesn't mean you suffer in silence. Often we keep things bottled up on the inside which usually shows up in others ways such as isolation, aggression and even depression. It's time to let it out.

Detach yourself from those who are hurting you no matter how much it hurts. It usually never hurts more than it does when you stick around. Also, sticking around ultimately says, "I love you more than I love myself." You can love others, but it should never cost you your peace, happiness or success. As a matter of fact, when you are surrounded by people who love you, they only want the best for you. A person who intentionally and continuously says and does things that they know are hurtful is emotionally abusive. It's not something to take lightly. Abuse isn't always physical. It can be verbal, emotional, psychological or sexual. Know that no matter what they say is the reason for their behavior, it is never your fault and should not be tolerated.

Declutter your physical space from items that trigger negative emotions. Sometimes we like to hold onto things that remind us of the good times, but often those same things serve as reminders of the bad times too. So if you're holding on to text messages, emails, letters, gifts or others trinkets- dispose of them in whatever way you see fit. Regift it, donate it, sell it or trash it. Just don't leave it sitting around waiting to set you off.

Detox with prayer, meditation, and journaling. At times like this, we need to connect with God on a deeper level. The occasional prayer of gratitude or special request won't cut it. You need to talk to God, pour your heart out and hand over your burdens. Meditate on scriptures that lift you up and leave you encouraged. Let them give you hope, strength, and peace. Write in a journal your thoughts and feelings. Do this daily as you develop the habit of detoxing from your day so you can let go and start fresh the next.

Protect your peace!

Session Three Declutter Your Spirit

When inner peace is missing... so is your relationship with God.

As you can see, clearing the clutter isn't done all on your own. And if you've been trying to do it that way, you're making it harder than it needs to be. You have a partner, a supporter, someone who has your best interest at heart, and that's God. There is absolutely no way I could have gone from clutter to clarity without Him. Honestly, I didn't really know much about God until my late 20s. As I started to learn more about Him, His Word and His promises, I started to transform and so did my life and relationships. But it wasn't at all what I had expected. I thought I would read the Bible, meet some good people at church, pray every day and boom - God would save me, bless me, and my life would be better. I learned quickly that God was not a genie in a bottle. I couldn't just rub him the right way (with my good deeds), and everything would work out perfectly. NO! Honestly, I barely knew what the Bible was saying half the time, I came across a lot of judgemental hypocrites, and I prayed out of desperation. I was still confused, hurting more, and less interested in being a Christian, so I went on sabbatical and connected with God on my own, my way. To this day, I believe this was just how He wanted me to get to know Him: through self-discovery and trial & error. I went out into the world, made a bunch of mistakes and revelation came every single time. And when I didn't learn, I would just experience the same thing again and again until I got it. God is the ultimate teacher, and we will forever be His students.

NO TEST, NO TESTIMONY.

When I was ready to fellowship, I met some awesome people who talked and taught about God in a way that made sense to me. It was real, raw and relevant. It resonated with me in a profound way. In a way that made me feel His approval and His love for me. It has been an amazing journey after all, and it continues to be. There are people out there who think they know it all, but they are still learning and growing in Christ too. Don't feel bad or behind because you're right where you're supposed to be in this season.

Speaking of seasons, you may be experiencing a tough one right now, but I want you to know that God is always available, day and night. You don't have to be perfect for Him to love you. You don't have to be the biggest giver for Him to bless you. You don't have to serve in your church 365 for Him to use you. Yes, you should do your best, be a cheerful giver and serve. However, that doesn't impress God. Your heart does. Your walk does. Your growth does. We don't deserve a thing, but He still wants to bless us and see us prosper. His love, grace, and mercy cannot be bought through tithes or volunteering. No matter how religious or righteous people seem, it's about the relationship, not religion. He wants a real relationship with you. Call on Him, love Him, trust Him, thank Him and give your unconditional love, even when you feel like He's nowhere around. Even when things aren't going right or when you don't feel like you can make it another day.

Our connection with God brings us peace, joy, and hope. Without that connection, we fall into dark places, deep depressions and vicious cycles that lead to dead ends. Realizing and releasing what is standing in the way of you having an amazing relationship with God gives Him the green light to begin unleashing your blessings and unblocking your breakthroughs. The problem is, a lot of what we have been taught about being Christians and how God sees us isn't always 100% accurate. So we end up in a slump of shame and guilt. We start to feel unworthy and disqualified. That usually leads to us isolating ourselves from God. And sadly, talking to the wrong believers could make you feel worse because not everyone speaking into your life is healed so they may be speaking from a place of pain. Be careful who you open up to.

ALWAYS SEEK WISE COUNSEL.

On this clutter free journey, I want you to always remember that God is who you answer to and who you should go to first. You don't have to go through life trying to figure things out all alone. He is your source, strength, and guide. Again, it is possible to attend church service every Sunday, bible study every Wednesday yet still not have a real relationship with God. You can quote scriptures all day and still feel empty and lost. But it doesn't have to be that way.

Always seek Him because He knows you best, knows your heart and knows your future. After consulting God is when you should seek wise counsel. God will lead you to the right person. Someone who will want to genuinely help you overcome your obstacles and will do so with love and understanding. Now, this doesn't mean you won't receive correction. That is a necessary part of the process. If you don't like others pointing out your ways, you're limiting what God can do in you and through them. Remain teachable, coachable and willing to do the work. Again, I stress WISE counsel. Not everybody who has a title is qualified to speak into your life. Seek God and ask for divine connections.

Next, keep your eyes, ears, and heart open. You will get supernatural clarity and build the unshakable confidence needed to pursue your purpose, reach your goals and live your dreams, but only when you let God lead. Learn to pray and be still. God won't always answer you right away, but if you are patient, he will answer. It won't always come in the form you expect, but it will come so stay expectant. Don't hand it over tonight and take it back tomorrow. Let go and let God.

Now, can I keep it real with you? I used to think that every time something didn't go right in my life it was either the enemy busy attacking me or God was punishing me. Whenever things didn't go my way or as planned, I blamed the enemy. I always thought he was messing with my money, interfering with my goals and hating on my relationships. But God revealed to me that He too would sometimes interfere by putting a stop to things that aren't good for us. Or maybe it wasn't bad per se, but He has something better. So I learned to embrace rejection as God's protection of me and the plans He has for me. I learned that He wasn't punishing me but pruning and preparing me for greater things. Know that all things are working out for your good even if it doesn't look good, sound good or feel good at the time.

When I got this revelation, my spirit was set free. I started to take ownership and responsibility for my decisions and actions (because sometimes WE are our own enemy) and I allowed God to be God. I stopped trying to be all, know all, and control all. And I tell what, it's such a great feeling not to carry all these burdens and fight all these battles.

I know I can't be alone in this. I think you've been guilty of blaming the devil for your decisions and questioning God about His. But if you want to shift from clutter to clarity spiritually and have more peace and joy, you have to get to know Him for yourself. There's nothing like it!

Who am I?

Let's shift gears for a second. Talking about decluttering your spirit excites me because when I started the process and cleared the clutter standing between God and me, I was able to discover who I was really created to be. That is a strong, powerful, virtuous woman. I want to share with you Proverbs 31. You probably already know and love it too, but I am sharing it here because this has really helped me stay focused on who I am as a woman and to seek God in moments where I was anything but virtuous and needed to get back on track.

Proverbs 31:10-31 King James Version (KJV)

10 Who can find a virtuous woman? for her price is far above rubies.
11 The heart of her husband doth safely trust in her, so that he shall have no need of spoil.
12 She will do him good and not evil all the days of her life.
13 She seeketh wool, and flax, and worketh willingly with her hands.
14 She is like the merchants' ships; she bringeth her food from afar.

15 She riseth also while it is yet night, and giveth meat to her household, and a portion to her maidens.

16 She considereth a field, and buyeth it: with the fruit of her hands she planteth a vineyard.

17 She girdeth her loins with strength, and strengtheneth her arms.

18 She perceiveth that her merchandise is good: her candle goeth not out by night.

19 She layeth her hands to the spindle, and her hands hold the distaff.

20 She stretcheth out her hand to the poor; yea, she reacheth forth her hands to the needy.

21 She is not afraid of the snow for her household: for all her household are clothed with scarlet.

22 She maketh herself coverings of tapestry; her clothing is silk and purple.

23 Her husband is known in the gates, when he sitteth among the elders of the land.

24 She maketh fine linen, and selleth it; and delivereth girdles unto the merchant.

25 Strength and honour are her clothing; and she shall rejoice in time to come.

26 She openeth her mouth with wisdom; and in her tongue is the law of kindness.

27 She looketh well to the ways of her household, and eateth not the bread of idleness.

28 Her children arise up, and call her blessed; her husband also, and he praiseth her.

29 Many daughters have done virtuously, but thou excellest them all.

30 Favour is deceitful, and beauty is vain: but a woman that feareth the Lord, she shall be praised.

31 Give her of the fruit of her hands; and let her own works praise her in the gates.

Moment of Clarity

What are the top 3 things cluttering your spirit right now?

In what ways do these things keep you spiritually disconnected?

Are you holding on to guilt, shame or fear that keeps you from connecting with God?

How will your life be different once your spirit is free and you are reconnected?

What actions can you take and are you willing to take NOW to remove these things that are creating spiritual clutter in your life so you can receive all that God has planned, prepared and promised you?

What does being a virtuous woman mean to you?

What changes can you start to make to get in alignment with the woman you were created to be?

Look good and feel better!

Session Four: Declutter Your Body

We've tackled the mind, emotions, and spirit. You had to know the body was next. Let me go ahead and put my disclaimer out there. This is an area of my life that I've always struggled with. But the more I became committed to living a clutter-free life, the less interested I was in doing things to my body that I would later regret. And I'm not just talking about struggles with food but casual sex, lack of exercise, negative self-talk and things that just are not conducive to honoring my body.

Healthy eating, staying hydrated, exercising and getting rest are all important factors to living a long, vibrant life. We all want to look good and feel good, however committing to the work involved in reaching our health and wellness goals can be challenging. It doesn't help that in today's society, it's all about quick fixes so everyone you see that looks good, isn't necessarily healthy. Being healthy is the ultimate goal. I want to help you discover any poor health habits and also help you eliminate them one day, one decision and one prayer at a time. Yes Lord, deliver us! Once you start to see the effects of how you've been treating your body, you will want to start making changes immediately. It's committing to those changes and being consistent in the day to day actions where most people fail.

I struggled with my weight as a kid. Growing up in a Hispanic household, at least two meals a day consisted of fried meat, rice, and beans. A lot of it too! It could have been fried pork chops, fried chicken or fried fish alongside fried plantains and a heap of white or yellow rice buried in beans. I loved every bit of it. I still do. What I don't love is how tired and lazy I would feel after I ate. After eating this way for years, I developed some unhealthy food habits. Portion control? What's that?! To make matters worse, nobody in my family exercised, so that was not something I was taught or inspired to do. I'm an introvert and don't like the heat, so playing outside wasn't my thing. I even got an F in physical education because I didn't want to participate. It was that bad.

So basically, I ate a lot and didn't move around much.

Over time, I gained excess weight and started to dislike my body. This is where my insecurities really started to kick in. Although we were all eating like this, my mom and sister maintained their small frames. Being that I am on the thicker side, I wasn't so lucky. I continued to gain weight. This is where the negative self-talk came into play. I would call myself fat on a daily basis. I would complain about my appearance and compare myself to other girls. Of course, I tried every diet on the market. I would lose weight then gain it all back- sometimes extra. And once I started having kids, it became harder to keep off. It wasn't until I realized the effect it was having in other areas of my life that I got serious about it.

If you constantly feel tired, sluggish and sleepy- those are signs that your body is cluttered and possibly has become toxic. If you don't feel comfortable wearing certain clothes, always pulling and tugging, hiding your body from your mate, comparing yourself to others and feel jealous or insecure, that body clutter has now become mental and emotional. If your self-esteem is low and you lack the courage to go after certain jobs or opportunities because of how you look and feel, that's clutter too, and now it's affecting your money. It's all clutter and clutter kills confidence!

Keeping things simple is what has helped my clients and me get results. Make small changes that work for your body and stick to them. Some simple changes I made were replacing white and yellow rice with brown rice. I replaced white bread with whole grain bread (not wheat). I eliminated red meat and pork and stuck to chicken, turkey, and fish. I only eat seafood now because I felt better when I eliminated meats altogether. I also have minimized my consumption of dairy and instead use almond milk, coconut milk, and other non dairy items when eating and cooking. Of course eating more fruits and veggies, drinking lots of water and decreasing processed and junk food was important too.

These changes over time, coupled with more movement has helped me shed some excess weight and increased my energy levels. Not to mention, my confidence increased as the weight decreased.

DON'T JUST LOOK GOOD, FEEL GOOD.

Now that is what works for me. You have to discover what works best for you. I am a believer in having a nutritionist and personal trainer on speed dial so you can ask questions and get a plan that works best for you. Everybody is different so what works for me may not work for you. Seek wise counsel from someone trained and certified to advise you in this area. Someone who can help you set realistic goals, map out your workouts and make suggestions for your meals. Get all the help you can in this area if it's a struggle because I guarantee you, it's affecting more of your life than you realize.

Here's the deal, this type of clutter isn't cleared by just eating better foods, exercising or becoming more confident. It's about learning to love yourself as is while you are working on being your best self. When I started my clutter free journey and began shedding the hurt and pain from my past, I started to see myself differently. I started to see myself as a strong and powerful woman regardless of my size. I started to see the woman God created me to be. I started to see my body as my temple. I started to see my lack of self-love and the effect it had on my body.

Quick Tips for Consistency

Schedule everything. Get your workouts on your calendar. Block off a time to exercise several days a week so you can create a consistent routine. Be it on your cell phone calendar or a planner, set your appointment with yourself and honor it.

Prep your meals. The easiest thing to do on a busy, chaotic or lazy day is to eat out. And unfortunately there's just not a lot of healthy fast food choices. Even the ones that we think are healthy aren't. So taking the time to cook and prep your meals for the week can save you time and money, not to mention unwanted weight.

Partner up. Find a reliable and committed friend who wants to live a healthy, fit lifestyle too and ask them to be your workout buddy. I go to the gym a couple of times a week with my best friend, and it helps us stay focused, motivated and consistent. She determines our cardio workout, and I decide on strength training. We keep it fun and fresh, so we never get bored. Plus, we can catch up on girl talk while we work out.

But, the truth is that's not even enough. See, the negative body images that many of us have are neither created in the kitchen nor will go away at the gym. These body issues are internal, both mental and emotional. You have to deal with why you're overeating, eating out of emotion, or not eating enough. You must get real and get to the root. It would have been easy for me to blame it on my upbringing. But what was my excuse long after I left my parent's house? I knew better, why wasn't I doing better? Because I didn't know that in order to heal my body I was going to have to heal my heart. Anger, bitterness, resentment, guilt, shame and so many other toxic feelings had become triggers for self-abuse, self-sabotage, and self-deprivation.

Emotional eating is very common and only deepens the wounds you want to heal. But in order to overcome you have to release that habit and replace it with a healthier one. So instead of grabbing food when you're feeling down- get up and get out. Do something more productive. That feeling won't last forever but the aftermath of your choices at the moment just might. It's ok not to be ok. I say, get in your feelings, then get out!

Move to Shift Your Mood

Movement. Get up and move. Staying stuck in the bed or on the couch is a no no. When you are physically still, your mind will race unless you're intentional with your thoughts, so move to shift your mood.

Music. This is my favorite way to get over my funk. Cut on your favorite songs, turn it up loud and jam. Sing, dance and have your own private concert. Music is made up of vibrations, and when your vibes are low, this is a way to get them up and out of the rut.

Meditation. If you're going to just sit there and think, you might as well be intentional about it. Meditate on scriptures, affirmations, and words that encourage and empower you. Don't just think about them, speak them. Your words have power so speak directly to your spirit and feel that burden lifted. This is also a good time to pray.

Messages. Listen to empowering messages via audio, video, podcast or grab an inspirational book to read. Let others pour into you when you can't pour into yourself. I start my day off with a good message because it sets the tone and my mood for the rest of the day.

Meet Ups. Get out the house and meet up with some friends, family or coworkers for a good time. Sometimes that change in environment and energy can help you realize that you are too blessed to be stressed.

You can have the body you want - tight, toned, sexy and energetic if (and only if) you are willing to start detoxing from the inside out. It takes time, commitment and consistency. It takes a plan and action. Set healthy body goals and work hard daily to reach them. Then work just as hard to maintain them. Stop the negative self-talk and be intentional about your self-care. And please do not compare yourself to others. You were fearfully and wonderfully made. God created you to be perfectly imperfect so that no one can compare to you. This is your journey! Focus on you!

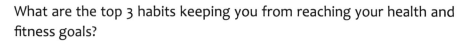

What are the top 3 habits keeping you from reaching your health and fitness goals?

In what ways do these things keep you from having the energy, body and confidence you want?

What decisions and distractions are present right now that are keeping you from reaching your fitness goals?

What are your specific fitness/health goals?

How will your life be different once you reach your health and fitness goals?

What actions can you take and are you willing to take NOW to get the results you desire?

Self love is the best love!

Session Five Declutter Your Relationships

I believe relationships have the power to influence and impact every area of your life. The people in your life are either helping you get ahead or keeping you stuck. This is why it is so important to take inventory of the people in your circle - friends, family, lovers - everybody. Those in whom you invest your time, money, energy and heart should be deserving. You must surround yourself with people who deserve to be in your life and who make valuable deposits not just withdrawals, leaving you depleted, exhausted and regretful.

I love talking about relationships and could write a whole book about it right now, but today I want to keep it super simple - STOP SETTLING FOR LESS.

When I say that to my clients, most of them think I'm just talking about the men or women in their lives. I'm not. I'm talking about everyone, including your family. Let's start there. Most people think that because they are family, they get some sort of pass. A pass that allows them to say and do whatever they want because they're blood, and "blood is thicker than water." Incorrect! As a matter of fact, because they are family, we typically have a higher expectation for them because we assume they all should love us, respect us, believe in us and support us. Again, incorrect. They don't owe you anything. And vice versa. Now some won't agree with me on this one, but those are usually the same people getting ran over or taking advantage of their family members.

Friendships are no different. Often people think because they are your friend, have known you a long time or have helped you out in the past that they get a pass too. Nope! No passes. I have ended friendships that were started over 20 years ago because we had outgrown each other or the relationship became toxic. As an adult, I realized that my relationships had the power to trigger things in me that I had worked too hard to overcome. When you like, love or care about someone, they affect you in ways that you can't always explain. This is why you should be careful who you entertain and only engage in healthy relationships. Real friendships aren't based on the length of time you've known someone. It's based on the love, respect, trust and loyalty you share. And that can come from someone new in your life. Of course, you should be cautious and not use the word friend lightly (which most people do) but give new people a chance to show you who they are because they just might have the personality and character that you have been expecting from your old friends.

Now you know I can't move on without touching on the primary relationship that gets us all caught up: Your lover. This bond is so powerful that it can make you feel like you're on cloud nine or like you're buried six feet deep. These are the relationships that make us feel like God loves us or like we're dancing with the devil. Here's the deal: No matter how much you love a person, you have to love yourself more. When you start to love others more than yourself, you tend to lose yourself in the relationship, and sometimes everything else. You must learn how to have healthy relationships that are built on respect, honesty, trust and loyalty. Anything else is settling for less. Anything else is tolerating someone who chooses to give little of themselves, and in my book, that's unacceptable.

Honestly, I LOVE love. I am a hopeful (not hopeless) romantic. I believe that when you have the right mate, you become a force to be reckoned with. Together you are a team and can conquer the world as long as you're not with someone trying to conquer you. What do I mean by that? Well, unfortunately, there are some people out there whose intentions are not right. They are deceitful opportunists who see you for what you have and what they can get. They may say all the right things and make you feel all the right ways, but eventually, their mask will come off, and the truth will be revealed. We know that the truth can hurt, but the truth can also set you free.

LOVE IS NOT BLIND, PEOPLE PRETEND TO BE.

I've coached many women who preferred to be in the dark so that they can avoid making the dreaded decision- to stay or go? So they ignore the signs, overlook the red flags, make excuses and justify the behavior of their partner, all because they don't want to be alone. I know that feeling you get when you realize your mate is not the one. That sick, sad, sunken feeling you get when the thought of starting over pops in your head. It's disappointing, devastating and even depressing when you know in your heart it's not going to work no matter how much you love them or how hard you try to fix it. The problem is, you can't fix people. You can't change them. They have to want to change, and until then, you'll catch hell.

Now hear me clearly, it's not all about you. Don't go into relationships only thinking of what you can get, but instead focus on what you can give. People always talk about what their mate needs to bring to the table but rarely check to confirm what they are bringing. No matter how cute, sexy or successful you are, if you are bringing drama, negativity, insecurities, jealousy, selfishness, judgment and all that other clutter to the table, nobody is trying to deal with that. This is why I stress the need to get yourself together mentally, emotionally, spiritually before you enter a relationship. Being financially secure is a great bonus, but it's not usually what will make your mate leave initially. It's all the internal baggage that takes a toll on us that leads us to not have patience in the other areas. So do the work required to heal and create happiness for yourself so you don't punish or pressure someone who could be your perfect match.

Be a person of value who makes their life happier, better and easier because you're in it. No, you are not responsible for their happiness, and they are not responsible for yours, but with the right person, you could be happier than ever before. That's why building a solid friendship first is crucial. It's something that needs to be established while dating before officially entering a relationship. So don't be in a rush. Trust me I know because I was the queen of rushing. I love fast, hard and deep, so I am speaking from experience. Take your time to build a real friendship and a solid foundation, so you're set up for success from the start. If he or she is the one, they're not going anywhere. As a matter of fact, they want to build something solid too. And no, there is not a set time frame for this to happen or for the relationship to move through the phases that lead to marriage. But what I will say is, know the difference between someone who has long term plans for you versus lifetime plans for you. Don't get stuck in a holding pattern with someone who is afraid of commitment or is nowhere near ready. Go live your life, and if they are the one, it will be.

YOU ARE WORTHY OF UNCONDITIONAL LOVE.

Never feel stuck or think you have to tolerate people's mess and mistreatment. You don't! You always have options. I'm a big believer in communication. If you are a passive person or a people pleaser, you may struggle with standing up for yourself and speaking your mind, but it's necessary. If you are one who always speaks your mind, remember that it's not always what you say but how you say it. Let them know upfront what your concerns are. Be honest but respectful. Watch your tone and body language. A lot of times, they may have a lot to say to you in return so be open to their feedback.

The truth is, sometimes a good talking to doesn't quite do the job. People will continue with their behaviors. So a little (or a lot) of distance between you may be the next best step. Space gives people time to think, reflect and feel - all of which are critical to making decisions. There's no magical time frame so let things flow. No need to beg them, chase them, or force them into change. Again, you can't change people. You can only control the way you react to them. They have to want to change, and that starts with them seeing the need to, which can come when they have the space to see their ways. Sometimes giving them space is not the solution. Sometimes you just have to press delete and let it go.

I believe people come into your lives for a reason, season or a lifetime. Holding onto people past their expiration date spoils everything. You have to understand that not all things are forever and that is actually for your good (and theirs!). Don't be afraid to end unhealthy, toxic, and dead-end relationships because they are truly costing you your peace, happiness and possibly your success. I know it's easier said than done, but it is doable. I know that it hurts- but so does staying. So do what you know you need to do- because we all know what we need to do even if we don't want to. Your relationships can be passionate, purposeful and prosperous if you are willing to shift them from clutter to clarity.

Moment of Clarity

What are the top 3 things cluttering your relationships with others right now?

In what ways do these things keep you from having happy, healthy, fulfilling relationships with people?

How will your life be different once your relationships with others are rekindled or released?

What actions can you take and are you willing to take NOW to revive, restore and rebuild your relationships?

In which relationships do you need to set boundaries?

Which relationships do you need to end completely?

Consider the type of friend you are and what your rating may be for others who share their space with you. Have the same expectations for yourself that you ask of them.

Your words have power!

Session Six Declutter Your Conversations

Believe it or not, the conversations you are having with yourself and others are either creating more of what you want or more of what you don't want. Your words have power! Every word you speak is a seed sown into a harvest to come. If you're planting seeds of fear, doubt, lack, anger, unforgiveness, loneliness, bitterness or brokenness, that is what will continue to grow in your life. It's time to start using your words in a more powerful, intentional and loving way.

As kids we were taught, "If you don't have anything nice to say, don't say anything at all." Although I think we all failed miserably at this, it is valuable advice. As tempting as it may be just to say whatever is on your mind or in your heart, you must be mindful that you are like a magnet that is always attracting something. What are you attracting? Is it negative energy, unhealthy relationships, or money problems? Is it health issues? Or is it the one thing that we often overlook - negative thoughts? Every time we say things like, "I'm so broke" or "I'm so fat" or "I hate my job," similar thoughts come following right behind them. And before you know it, you're an hour into your pity party and feel even worse than when you started. Depending on who you're talking to, they may make matters worse by agreeing with you or dumping their baggage onto yours. Now you're stressing over your crap and theirs too. Plus, who wants to be around all that negativity? People who let you sit around and carry on like this do so because it agrees with their situation. Misery loves company.

It has become so common for people to complain to friends and family, but now that social media is so readily available, they are comfortable complaining to complete strangers. They post how they are feeling about their life, relationship, job, finances, and friendships, often looking for attention, agreement or sympathy. But what they didn't expect was feedback, opinions, and judgment. We have all seen the drama in the comments section, but that can be avoided. Share what you want people to know and never forget. What do I mean by that? Always keep in mind that what you share today remains long after you're over the situation so if you don't want to be reminded or judged by your post or your past, keep people out of your business. Don't invite people into your issues unless they can help you solve them.

WATCH YOUR MOUTH.

Because you've probably been speaking like this, privately or publicly, for some time, it's going to take practice to change it. Negative self-talk, complaining and gossip easily becomes a habit that most people have and don't necessarily think they need to change. They just don't see how it's impacting their lives or the lives of others, but it is. Don't get me wrong, even those who are super conscious will slip up from time to time. It's called being human. However, we should be striving to be better and do better, so understanding the power of your words can help you shift from clutter to clarity. This will allow you to use your words to attract and create a life you love.

I grew up around a lot of cluttered conversations, so I became immune to all the yelling, cursing, gossiping, judging and complaining. As I got older and became exposed to teachings like what I'm sharing with you, I became aware of the role I was playing in the struggles I was experiencing. After I had started to become more conscious of my conversations and more intentional with my words, I couldn't stand being around people who spent the whole time being negative. I'm not talking about a healthy venting session with a good friend, supportive family member, your pastor or a life coach, because holding everything in isn't healthy either. I'm talking about people who have no desire to solve any of their problems. They just want to talk about them to anybody who will listen. That's unhealthy, unproductive and unattractive.

SPEAK FROM A PLACE OF POWER.

Despite your situation or circumstances, you can learn to speak from a place of power. A simple adjustment of your words can greatly adjust your mindset and mood. Do you say affirmations? I love affirming what I want versus confirming what I lack. Using affirmations is a great way to call forth what you desire. It's a great way to encourage and empower yourself. It's a great way to stay focused on what you want to attract and create. You can use "I AM," "I CAN," and "I WILL" in your statements rather than "I'M NOT, "I CAN'T" or "I WON'T."

Some of my favorites are:

I AM CLEAR, CONFIDENT AND COURAGEOUS.
I AM WHOLE AND COMPLETE.
I AM STRONG AND POWERFUL.
I AM ENOUGH.
I AM WANTED, NEEDED AND NECESSARY.
I AM THE SOLUTION.
I CAN DO ALL THINGS THROUGH CHRIST WHO STRENGTHENS ME.
I CAN CONQUER ANYTHING AND EVERYTHING.
I CAN MAKE A DIFFERENCE.
I WILL REACH ALL MY GOALS.
I WILL LIVE MY DREAMS.
I WILL WIN IN ALL AREAS OF MY LIFE.

During a recent coaching session, I shared how to shift from venting to victory with my client who is working on emotional healing. A major part of the healing process is to be able to discuss your past and your pain with power. Although you may be tempted to vent while expressing yourself, I encourage you to claim victory over your healing and speak from a place of authority. That means you are not just sharing your story. You are sharing your testimony, even if you are still in the process of overcoming the obstacles. Confess and claim it! When you speak with this level of clarity, you can encourage and empower others instead of joining their pity parties or inviting them to yours.

EVEN WHEN YOU FEEL POWERLESS, YOUR WORDS STILL HAVE POWER.

I must repeat, reciting affirmations and positive thinking aren't enough. It will make you feel better but won't make your life any better if you don't take action on a grand scale that is consistent. That is what will lead to the change you want to see in your life. So use the power of your words and make moves!

One powerful way to shift your conversations is to ask yourself questions. Instead of saying, "I'm broke," you can ask yourself, "Why don't I have enough money?" Or instead of saying, "I'm not happy." you can ask yourself, "Why am I unhappy?". Asking yourself questions can only lead to one thing - answers. Those answers can lead to breakthroughs. So, get into the habit of asking yourself questions that will cause you to shift from problem to solution.

When all else fails, practice silence. Most people struggle with silence because silence gives you room to think. And if you think long enough, your stuff will show up. A lot of people don't want to deal with their stuff, so they create noise and distractions instead. If you find yourself in a mental space where all you are doing is nagging and being negative, be still and be quiet. No tv, no radio, no cell phone, no tablets, no laptops or computers. Nothing but you and God. Talk to Him. Express your feelings to Him. Ask Him questions. And wait for His reply. The answers to your prayers may not come immediately, but they will come if you submit your request and remain open to receiving what God wants to show you.

Moment of Clarity

What are the top 3 conversations you are having with yourself or others that could be blocking your blessings and breakthroughs?

How have you received exactly what you spoke through negative conversations with yourself and others? Be honest; think about what you have said that could have created the clutter in your life right now.

What words have you spoken that you want to ask God to cancel right now?

What positive, life-affirming words can you speak that will send out a clear message to attract, create and manifest what it is you truly desire for your life?

Create personal affirmations to recite every single day. Write several affirmations below then transfer them onto sticky notes, index cards, in a journal or any place you will see them throughout the day and say them every chance you get.

My Daily Affirmations

You have to BE and DO before you can HAVE!

Session Seven: Declutter Your Finances

To reach a place of financial freedom is a goal that everyone has but it's not a goal everyone will accomplish if they aren't aware of their money mindset, mistakes and the steps to money mastery. Knowing where you stand financially and the money habits that you have will bring the needed clarity to make changes and better decisions when it comes to your finances.

Some people were lucky enough to be taught about the value of money, saving, investing and giving early on. Others, like myself, had to learn the hard way - through trial and error. So I am passionate about helping people, especially women, understand the power of financial clarity and freedom.

I didn't "come from money." My parents worked very hard to survive, but we never had extra to live on. That's how it was for everyone around me, so initially, it wasn't an issue. I just didn't know what I didn't know. However, once I reached high school and was exposed to kids who lived in nicer homes, drove nice cars, and went on family vacations- I knew there was more to life than just paying bills. I wanted to go to the movies on the weekend, go shopping at the mall, and do other fun activities with my friends without having to hear complaints whenever I asked. I know now that those complaints were just reactions to my parents own frustrations about not having more money.

Over time, I became that same way, working hard to make just enough to get by. Being a single mom didn't make things easier either. I've made a lot of mistakes with money over the years. One of the biggest lessons that I've learned was that in order to get my money right, I needed to my mind right. I was so focused on lack and limits that I didn't see the possibilities of prosperity.

THE ONLY LIMITS IN LIFE ARE THE ONES YOU PLACE ON YOURSELF.

Money problems don't just affect your bank account. They affect many areas of your life. Many relationships end because of money issues. Many people stay stuck in jobs they hate because of their money issues. Some people never get out, travel or even visit family far away because of money issues. And some people never reach their goals or live their dreams because of money issues. The truth is, it's not really the money that's the problem. It's their mindset, beliefs, and habits with money that is the real issue. I've helped several clients fix their finances by simply helping them see that focusing on the money they didn't have wasn't going to give them the money they needed. Some realized that their job alone would never be enough money to cover all their bills and they needed more income or multiple streams of income, which I believe everyone should have anyway. Some clients realized that not aggressively tackling their credit card debt was keeping them stuck and if they would just bite the bullet and send more or pay them off sooner, they would have more than enough for the bills each month. Others realized that they did earn enough money, but their spending habits were the real issue. Money is flowing in your life but what are you doing with it?

A lot of people feel like because they work so hard, they should be able to spend what they want and when they want. But the truth is that if you are behind on bills and living check to check, getting out of that vicious cycle should be the priority, not going to the mall or the club or the restaurants. It doesn't matter how hard you have worked. Yes, you worked hard and can treat yourself here and there, but when you become really committed to fixing your finances, you will want to make the necessary sacrifices to get to your goal. Sacrifice is not a negative word like most people think. It is a mature way of saying "I'm going to do what I have to do now to have the things I want to have later."

God wants us to be good stewards of our money. He wants us to live abundant lives. Yes, financially as well as the other areas of our lives. It's hard to feed, clothe and shelter those in need if we don't have anything to give, so why not do the work, make money and be in the position to bless others? We were not created to live in lack. That doesn't glorify God or help build his kingdom. So, getting your money right needs to become a priority. Reciting money affirmations and reading prosperity books aren't going to cut it. You have to do the work by putting your God-given gifts and talents to use. I believe that God has already given us what we need to be financially free but not everyone is tapping into it. If you look around at many of the successful people you admire who are wealthy, you will probably notice they are using what they are good and gifted at to generate income. It could be in a career or business, but nevertheless, they are putting in work and reaping the benefits. These are usually the same people who are also givers. They are the ones who understand they are blessed to be a blessing.

MASTER YOUR MONEY; DON'T LET IT BECOME YOUR MASTER.

Another mindset shift that needs to take place is thinking you are forever indebted to or obligated to help people who have helped you in the past. I'm not saying to stay on the receiving end and never give, but make sure you are giving what you can afford to give just in case you never get it back. You have to learn how to say no without feeling guilty when you really can't help. Just because you have, it doesn't mean you should give it.

I have been guilty of this for years. Certain people who have declared me Bank of Angel and come to make withdrawals after they have blown their paychecks. I can't blame them because I allowed it to happen for years. Each time they would borrow money, or I would pay their bills, they would get paid and spend their money without consideration of repaying me. They would even have the audacity to tell me they had to take care of their new bills and responsibilities and will pay me back when they could as if I didn't have responsibilities of my own. I would get so angry and say that it was the last time, but guess what? I did it over and over again until I realized how they weren't the problem. I was. I realized the love they had for me wasn't really for me but the benefits. It was a hard pill to swallow, but I did. I decided I wouldn't allow it anymore. It was one of the best decisions ever.

Did you know that you can also become the source of someone else's financial problems when you enable their behaviors? This causes them not to prioritize their money because they know they can just call on you. You become their solution to a problem that they have no intentions on fixing. When you become committed to getting your financial house in order, you will realize that overspending and over-sharing has to stop. It is not only hurting you, but it's hurting them. You must understand that they won't like it. They will get mad about your money. They will say things to make you feel bad or guilty. They will act as if you've never helped them at all. That's ok. Let them get in their feelings. It will only reveal who they truly are and how they really feel.

BELIEVE WHO PEOPLE ARE, NOT WHO YOU WANT THEM TO BE.

Do yourself a favor and focus on your money goals and be willing to do whatever it takes (legally of course) to get to where you want to be financial. Use your gifts, talents, skill set and passions to generate multiple streams of income, so you aren't dependent on one way to get paid. I used my education to start my tutoring company to supplement my income. I used my gift as a teacher to create an online classroom to educate, encourage and empower women. I used my gift of communication to work my network marketing business selling health products. I used my passion for writing to get this book in your hand. I used what God gave me to create financial freedom, and you should too!

There's nothing wrong with working for a company, but there's nothing like having your own company. Honestly, I don't think everyone was created to be an entrepreneur. Somebody has to answer the phones, clean the buildings, cook the food, teach the kids, etc.

But, if you're one of those people who likes to march to the beat of your own drum, hate taking orders from the higher ups, want to schedule out your own day , like wearing jeans during the week, and don't like limits when it comes to your income potential...you probably were designed to be your own boss.

As a classroom teacher, I never thought of being my own boss. I went to school, got my education and got a good job just like I was told. But God had other plans that weren't yet revealed to me. So I taught for years before I recognized the entrepreneur in me. But once I did, it was on!

Even after shutting down my tutoring business, that tug at my heart to do my own thing was still there. It never left. Eventually, I answered the call. But I must let you in on a secret. I didn't really want to do the hard work of building my own business from scratch, so I sought out opportunities to "be my own boss" through network marketing. I kept teaching but had a new side hustle. I learned so much from my training and grew as a person tremendously, but I realized that although I was my own boss, it was still not my business. I didn't own the company and should that company shut down, so would my ability to make money through that vehicle.

I cannot stress this enough- if you work for a network marketing company, find additional ways to use that platform to build something of your own. Become an author, a speaker, a brand so that you can say something is 100% yours. Because I had access to so many women, I made sure to connect with them and found out how else I could help them win in life. This is what truly led me to becoming a life coach. I still worked the business and eventually joined a new company that was more in alignment with the brand I created. I wanted to keep that stream of income while having one that I could call my own: H.O.T Coaching, which is short for Helping Others Transform.

Maybe you want to climb the corporate ladder. Climb it!

Maybe you want a new job. Get it!

Maybe you want to write a book. Write it!

Maybe you want to launch your own business. Start it!

Whatever it is you want to do, do it now!

Moment of Clarity

What are the top 3 reasons you are not where you want to be financially?

What are some of the things you are spending money on each month that is not a necessity? Be specific. NOTE: Investments give you something of lasting value in return, spending does not.

What money habits do you have that are causing you to waste or lose money that could be invested or used to create financial freedom?

What new money habits are you going to start implementing so you can save, invest and have financial peace?

What are some ways you can decrease your current expenses (such as cutting off the cable, choosing a cheaper cell phone plan, eating out less, paying cash, paying in full)?

What are some ways to decrease your debts quickly that will increase your credit score?

What are some ways to increase your income (such selling unwanted items online, working overtime, finding a side hustle, starting your own business)?

Less is more!

Session Eight Declutter Your Environment

You knew this time would come, right? Well, it's here. We are going to clean out the physical clutter in your life and create space for creativity, peace, and positive energy to flow. The clutter we see around us is the manifestation of the clutter within us. No matter how hard you try to hide it, the confusion and chaos in your life, relationships or work will begin to show itself in the physical. When you tackle your physical space, you are clearing out your mental and emotional space as well. Getting your life organized starts with organizing the places you spend the most time, such as your home, car, and office. Over time, the more you do the inner work, the less outter work will be needed.

I once ended a toxic relationship, which resulted in me going through depression. I remember how my room became a disaster. The rest of my house was clean because my kids were good about keeping up with their chores, but my bedroom was my responsibility. My bed had piles of clean clothes that needed to be folded and put away, stacks of mail sat on the dresser that needed to be opened, and my student's papers were scattered on the floor, waiting to be graded. It was clear that my recent break up was taking a toll on me mentally, emotionally and physically. One Friday, I looked around my room and thought to myself, "This is a damn shame. I can't spend another day living like this!" The mess was adding to the stress, so I began to sort through the mail, fold the clothes and graded all the papers. I was up all night getting my room together. That Saturday morning I woke up the kids, put on some reggae music and we did a deep cleaning of every room in the entire house including the garage.

We spent the whole weekend decluttering, and it felt great. I was no longer focused on my past hurt but my future happiness. A weight had been lifted, and an internal shift had taken place. As I cleared the clutter on the outside, I was clearing the clutter on the inside. Make keeping your house clean and orderly a priority, especially if you are asking God for a new home, a bigger home, or a better home. Take care of what you have, so he can trust you with what he has for you.

Your home is your sanctuary. Keep it clean, organized and clutter-free. I am providing you with a list of things you can work on to clear the clutter in your physical space.

YOU ARE GOING TO "CLEAN OUT".

To clean UP leaves you with all the same stuff that ends up out of place again. It is more effective and productive to clean OUT so you can make room for new things to come into your life.

Don't go at it alone though. Get your girlfriend, boyfriend, best friend, children or whoever to help so you can speed up the process. Now understand, you didn't create this clutter overnight so do not expect it to be gone overnight.

I would encourage you to spend an hour or two each day over the next few weeks to get it all cleared out while you are getting clear in other areas of your life.

Continue the cleansing process when you have moments to spare. Tackle one area at a time to avoid being overwhelmed. Prioritize areas that need attention immediately like common areas versus those that can wait like the unseen areas.

Call your helpers now and make arrangements for them to assist you on a day and time that is convenient for them, however, do not wait for their help to get started. This is YOUR responsibility, so no excuses!

When your home is in order put some routines and systems in place, so it stays that way. Have a family meeting and assign (or reassign) chores. Make sure everyone is held accountable for keeping their personal spaces clean and contributing to the common areas.

Even if you are a stay at home wife or mom, just because you have the time doesn't mean you should spend it all on cleaning. Get everyone on board and make your life easier. If you are single, check yourself and determine why you are allowing your home to be cluttered. Chances are, it's an inner issue that needs to be addressed. It could have just become a bad habit of not keeping house, and that can change simply by establishing routines and clean up days and sticking to it.

Lastly, don't be afraid of hiring help. If you can afford it, do it! This doesn't make you lazy. It's actually a smart decision because that time you would have spent cleaning, you could have spent working on your goals.

Just think about the peace of mind and free time you will have when you don't have to spend it searching through the clutter and cleaning up constantly.

You can do this.

Start today!

Moment of Clarity

Which are areas of your home that are currently cluttered?

Do you have clothes, items, food, etc. that could be discarded or donated? If yes, where can you take them?

Do you need help to tackle your clutter or can you get the job done alone?

Who can you rely on to assist you through this process that will not judge, criticize or complain? Do you need to hire a cleaning service?

Clutter Free Checklist

Kitchen
- ☐ Cabinets & Pantry
- ☐ Appliances (stove, oven, refrigerator, microwaves)

Living room/Den
- ☐ Organize or get rid of CDs, DVDs, and anything else that is broken, missing, or unused. Organize cords to tv, cable, speakers, video games, etc.

Bathroom
- ☐ Throw out any old, unused toiletries
- ☐ Organize items you keep
- ☐ Throw out expired medicine
- ☐ Clean out makeup bag LADIES!
- ☐ Replace worn towels and wash cloths

Closets
- ☐ Clean out and donate clothes that are too big, too small, and outdated

Office
- ☐ Sort through papers and throw out/shred unwanted documents
- ☐ Organize files, books, items on desk
- ☐ Organize important documents like life insurance, policies, mortgage papers, etc.
- ☐ Clean out your computer. Get rid of documents, images, and videos you no longer need.
- ☐ Throw out old billing statements, checkbooks, and anything else that you haven't looked at this past year.

Bedroom
- ☐ Get rid of old, faded, torn, stained sheets and deflated pillows
- ☐ Organize dresser drawers
- ☐ Take anything work related to your office or another space (your room is your sanctuary, not office)
- ☐ Kid Rooms- All of the above as well as donate unused toys and clothes, throw out broken toys
- ☐ Organize accessories, LADIES!!!

Overall Cleaning
☐ Dust all rooms
☐ Sweep & mop
☐ Clean baseboards
☐ Clean Blinds
☐ Clean windows
☐ Clean ceiling fans
☐ Clean air filters
☐ Paint or touch up walls
☐ Shampoo carpet

Garage/Storage
☐ Donate the items you placed in the garage and never gave away
☐ Organize tools on a rack or shelf
☐ All equipment, toys, etc. should be with like items and neatly stored
☐ Out of season items to be placed in attic, basement, or storage shed
☐ Sweep and mop if applicable

Yard
☐ Cut grass
☐ Pull weeds
☐ Sweep/blow walkway and driveway
☐ Clean pool
☐ Organize items in yard

Vehicle
☐ Throw out any trash
☐ Vacuum
☐ Shampoo seats and carpet
☐ Dust /wipe down interior
☐ Wash exterior
☐ Clean out trunk

The sky is not the limit!

Session Nine Declutter Your Habits

As I shared earlier, your thoughts become feelings, your feelings become words, your words become actions, your actions become habits and habits create your reality. To create a shift in your life, you have to start with what you do daily. Changing habits isn't always easy, but it's always worth it when you understand that YOU have created the life that you are living, and you have the power to create a better one with your thoughts, words, and actions.

Whether it is overeating, excessive spending, gossiping, lying, cheating, procrastinating, and every other bad habit you can imagine, they all started with one action that was repeated over and over until it became your new bad habit. But there is hope. Just as we can quickly create a bad habit, we can replace it with a good habit through the power of repetition. Repetition creates results. You can develop new habits that can help make your life easier and better if you just commit to changing them one habit at a time.

Although habits come from repeated actions, they are often a manifestation of a deeper issue. I remember a simple habit I had developed in my teens that lasted through my 20's. It put my insecurities on front street. Every time a woman gave me a compliment, I would come back with something to downplay it. If they told me I looked nice, I would say, "Not as nice as you." If they told me they loved my earrings, I would say, "They only cost $1." Or, if they would tell me I did a great job, I would respond with, "I could have done better." I didn't know how to receive compliments. I would even feel obligated to give one in return even if it wasn't true.

Then one day an older lady I worked with complimented me on my dress and before I could give a rebuttal she said, "Just say thank you." Honestly, I was a little offended. I replied, "I was going to say thank you, but you didn't give me a chance." She explained to me that she noticed

I could never just say thank you and needed to stop acting insecure. Wow. Now I was really getting pissed off. I'm not insecure! Although I was. Very insecure actually. So downplaying, shrinking back and dimming my light had become habits that everyone saw except me. Seems harmless, right? However, it was reinforcing low self-esteem and self-worth.

YOU ARE DEFINED BY YOUR HABITS.

Even though I didn't want to agree with this woman, she was right. This led me to think about how all my other habits and ways of being was creating this perception of me that I didn't want people to have, especially my co-workers. No matter what your habits are, the negative ones run deep. Retail therapy and overeating are habits many women have to avoid dealing with their stress and struggles or disappointments and depression. Having casual sex with random people is another habit many women have to avoid dealing with their trust issues and insecurities. I know these habits very well because they once were mine. I was guilty of behaving in this careless way. So creating better habits can help get rid of the hidden clutter that may not be at the forefront of your mind but is showing up in various areas of your life. We can't always see our ways, but they are always on display.

To begin the process of changing your habits, I want you to try my release and replace method. When trying to change their habits, people start off strong but tend to fall off quickly. What I teach my clients to do is for every habit you want to release, think of a new habit you can replace it with. For example, instead of laying on the couch binge watching the latest Netflix series while munching on potato chips, you can get up to prep your meals and workout or jot down some new goals and get started on them right away. We complain that there is not enough time in the day to get everything done, but with habits like laziness and procrastination, that's simply not true. We all have the same 24 hours in a day. It is our choice to use our time wisely. Successful people maximize their time, energy, money and resources. Excuse makers with bad habits never do.

They say it takes 21-30 days of consistent action to create the new habit so don't rush the process. Give yourself time to develop new habits. You must also give yourself some grace. You won't always get it right. You may fall short. They goal is to try not to but if you do, don't beat yourself up. Beating yourself up doesn't change anything, becoming better does.

Helpful Habits to Have

Establish routines. Routines are the things we do day to day that doesn't require much thought. They tend to happen naturally once established like waking up, brushing your teeth, washing your face and getting dressed. But there are other actions you can add to your routine to set yourself up for success like watching an empowerment video while eating breakfast or listening to personal development audios while you drive to work. This gives you a chance to get motivated and inspired before you get to work, setting a positive tone for your day.

Develop rituals. Rituals are like routines in that they happen daily. However, they are more intentional and intrinsically motivated actions that impact the way you feel. Not all rituals are spiritual, but having spiritual rituals can help keep you feel connected to God, grounded and a sense of peace. One of my morning rituals is to say a prayer before I sit up. Then I get out of bed and slowly stretch to wake my body up. I head to the kitchen to fix myself a cup of hot lemon water and/or hot tea, and I recite a few affirmations while it's preparing. I then come back to my bed and cuddle under my blanket with my drink in one hand and an inspirational book in the other. I read while I slowly sip my drink. Once I finish, I get my journal and jot down my goals for the day and begin to wake up my children for school. This may sound like a routine but what makes it a ritual is that I am intentional about nurturing and feeding my mind, body, and spirit before I nurture anyone else. It's sacred me time and it's non-negotiable.

Pray often. Prayer can be as simple as having a conversation with God. There is no right or wrong way to pray. There is no right or wrong time to pray. You can speak to God at any time throughout your day - verbally or mentally - about whatever is on your mind and heart. Often guilt, shame and a lack of faith keep us from connecting with God through prayer. So it's important to release that spiritual clutter, so there is nothing separating you from the source. There are specific types of prayer such as:

Prayer of agreement
Prayer of faith
Prayer of consecration and dedication
Prayer of intercession
Prayer of binding and loosing
Prayer of praise and worship

You can research and learn more about each one, however, do not get caught up in the details. Use the power of prayer to speak life over and into situations you want to see changed. God is always available. Seek Him, and seek Him FIRST. He's not looking for perfection, but connection.

ASK. BELIEVE. RECEIVE.

Meditate daily. Meditation is a powerful way to start and end your day. It is also a great way to check back in mentally when you find yourself stressed, overwhelmed or unfocused. Making this a daily habit will help you to be more calm and collected which leads to more peace and happiness. Meditation also helps increase clarity which will positively affect your confidence and decision making. There are many different types of meditations you can research but what I would like to recommend is that you start by meditating on God's word. Pick a scripture that speaks to you and read it. Recite it. Study it. Meditate means to think deeply and carefully about something. Let that "something" be God's word and will for your life.

Visualize daily. Spend at least 5 minutes each morning visualizing your day. Envision your day going smoothly and successfully. Picture yourself reaching your goals and living your dreams. See yourself living the life you desire. You can do this during your meditation time or you can spend some time visualizing with your vision board, vision wall or vision book. These are tools that you can use to help you see the things you want mentally before they show up physically. If you aren't into vision boards and such but like to get techy, you can also create your vision video comprised of pictures, words, and sounds that inspire you. I also love creating inspiration boards and brand boards for my business. It's important to keep your goals and dreams in front of you, especially when things in your life are not going so well because it keeps you focused. The goal here is to spend time seeing in your mind what you want to see in your life. And when you do this daily, it increases your faith and focus.

Exercise regularly. Movement is key to not only looking good but also feeling good. Maybe you already love working out and are fully committed or maybe you were about to skip this part but your gut told you to come back and read it. Exercise doesn't have to be strenuous however it does need to get your heart rate up. Try cardio for 30 minutes a day and strength training at least twice a week. You don't need a gym! For most healthy adults, the changes in your body, energy levels and confidence will be significant.

Eat healthily. Eating healthy doesn't mean depriving yourself of foods you enjoy, it simply means finding new ways to eat them that are healthier for your body. That means enjoying more wholesome foods like vegetables, fruits, and whole grains, plus healthy proteins and fats. It also means limiting refined grains, pesticides, additives, preservatives, unhealthy fats and large amounts of sugar and salt. By making these changes, one day at a time, you will begin to see the benefits. Some of the benefits include clear, radiant skin and a fit, energetic body. Who doesn't want that? If you've been struggling with eating clean for some time, be patient. It's going to take time to change your habits. And remember, it's a not a quick fix, it is a lifestyle change. Avoid fad diets, pills, and other gimmicks. Do what it takes to create a healthy habit. Progress over perfection!

Read more. Making reading a habit changed my life. Although I was an elementary school teacher for 13 years, I didn't read anything outside of mandatory readings for teachers. What I discovered is that I had access to life changing information that contained the answers to my questions, the solutions to my problems, the steps to my breakthrough, but I wasn't taking advantage of it. Reading quickly became a non-negotiable habit. I now read self-help, inspirational and business books weekly to stay informed, inspired and empowered. Commit to reading books that are relevant to your goals, dreams, and desires for at least 15 minutes a day. It can have a positive influence and impact on your mindset, emotions, and decisions. Reading has the power to help you discover new things about yourself, other people, and more. Add this to your morning or evening routines so you can start thinking and living outside of the box. Highlight passages, take notes and implement what you learn.

Start journaling. There's something powerful about putting pen to paper. You can journal about your thoughts, feelings, goals, dreams, and desires. You can write out "to do" lists, action plans, ideas, affirmations and more. Journaling allows you to declutter your mind of all these things so you can be free, focused and productive on a daily basis. One of my obsessions is beautiful journals. I have so many in different colors, patterns, and sizes. I love them all. Head out today and grab yourself a few. You can use one for goals and dreams, one for prayers, affirmations and gratitude, one for business, one for personal development, or you can include all that goodness in one special journal. It doesn't really matter as long as you start expressing yourself and decluttering your mind. All of my clients and Clutter Free Society members have journals. Get one!

Set goals. Most likely, you already set goals, but SMART goals require more intention. SMART stands for Specific, Measurable, Attainable, Relevant, and Time-based. This is great for your annual, quarterly and even monthly goals, but I highly recommend you get in the habit of setting daily goals as well. This is more than just a "to do" list. This is setting specific goals for the day that your time and attention will go to first. These are your top priorities and should tie into your bigger SMART goals. They are NOT just tasks but goals that contribute to a bigger cause. You can jot these down in the morning or the night before, so you wake up prepared and ready to start your day with intention. Your goals will help create your to-do list. Don't keep them in your head. Write them down and check them off. By the end of each day, you'll feel successful and closer to your dreams.

Take action. Now that you have your goals down- get going! Take action every single day so you can get further faster. You don't just want to become busy doing stuff, but instead doing the things that matter most. You want to be purpose driven and productive daily. Having clear goals and your tasks written out will help you do just that. But having it all written isn't enough. You need to be intentional about eliminating distractions. Cell phones, social media, and television are the top three time wasters that will prevent you from reaching your goals each day. I'm not saying that you can't have a social life or kick back and relax with your favorite show. Just save those things until your work is done. If you want to get more done in less time, you have to get laser focused. You can schedule what I call Power Hours and work in 60-minute sessions with small breaks in between if needed. This will help keep you on track so you can achieve more and feel that amazing sense of accomplishment that will serve as motivation for the next day. Don't just take action. Take massive action! Go big. Go hard. Do more. Give it your all.

Get rest. At the end of the day, your body needs rest. No matter how much of a go-getter you are, you need rest. The average adult needs between seven and nine hours of sleep. Many can function on much less but don't necessarily operate at their best. While you are sleeping your body is recovering, renewing and rejuvenating itself in preparation for the next day. If you lack energy, focus or the motivation to go after your goals, get some rest! And don't feel guilty. That "I'll sleep when I die" mentality sounds good, but the more organized, intentional, and productive you are, the less guilty you'll feel about going to bed.

Those are some habits that myself and my clients stick to because they make a huge difference in the way we think, feel, speak and act. These are habits of the successful and you deserve to be among them. One of my favorite quotes by motivational speaker Les Brown is, "In order to have what others don't, you have to do what others won't." When I heard that statement, it was like a smack in the face. I was so used to following the crowd that I didn't realize that was the reason I wasn't getting anywhere. The crowd didn't know where they were going. They were lost; The blind leading the blind. We were all doing the same thing and in turn dealing with the same struggles and getting nowhere fast.

CHANGE YOUR HABITS, CHANGE YOUR LIFE.

Moment of Clarity

What are your top 3 habits that are preventing you from reaching your goals and living your dreams?

What are other habits getting in your way of success (such as making excuses, procrastination, blaming others, etc.)?

What helpful habits could you replace those with (such as being committed, consistent, optimistic, taking action, doing it afraid, etc)?

What top 5 habits do you need to possess to be more, do better and have the best (think opposite of the habits holding you back)?

Make the vision plain!

Session Ten Clarify Your Vision

Having a vision for your life is key to creating a life you love. You have to see it mentally before you can see it manifest. Most people say "I'll believe it when I see it" however you won't see it until you truly believe it is possible. Your current vision is most likely made up of your desires, your past experiences and your current circumstances plus what others have suggested. Depending on what has occurred in your past and what you're dealing with today, you may not be seeing all the possibilities that lie ahead. This is why decluttering your vision today is needed. Getting all those other areas of your life decluttered is cool, but it's not the "end all be all." It's time to LIVE your life!

You wouldn't believe how many women and men I work with who come to me because they do not have a vision for their life. They don't know what they DO want because they are so focused on what they don't want. They don't dream anymore because they have accepted their current circumstances as their reality. They stopped setting goals because they stopped believing in themselves. And they stopped enjoying life because life has no meaning to them. This is why I am stressing that having a life vision is important. As a matter of fact, it is non-negotiable! It gives life real meaning and purpose. It provides you with something to look forward to. It also gives you hope. So I want to help you clarify your life vision so that you aren't stuck, settling or simply existing. You deserve better than that.

LIFE IS MEANT TO BE LIVED.

A few years ago, I started a practice to help me in this area. I started making time to visualize, meditate, journal and pray every morning. A lot of people do one or more of these from time to time, but creating consistency and a routine is powerful. Doing this in the morning before you get your day started is helpful because it allows you to focus your mind and set your intentions before you let in the drama of the day. It only takes about 15 minutes, but sometimes I spend up to an hour in this mental space. You can get so caught up you just don't want to stop dreaming. Don't worry about setting a timer or become rigid in this practice- let it flow, so it feels good when you do it.

Start off by visualizing your dream life. This is the life you would be living if you had a magic wand and could make all your dreams come true today. This is the life that makes you so happy all you can do is smile just thinking about it. It makes you feel excited, free and fulfilled. It makes you feel alive. This is the life you would live if nothing and no one were stopping you.

Now start to narrow that vision. Slowly bring it into the year, then the month, then week and finally the day you want to create for yourself. I do it this way because when you start by just visualizing your day, you're most likely going to become overwhelmed with your responsibilities instead of the possibilities. So fill yourself up with positive, inspiring and motivating images first and then carry them into your day.

Having a vision board can help with this phase because sometimes we need to see it with our eyes before we can see it in our mind. And that's ok. If you're not a fan of vision boards, that's ok too. I just want you to become committed to visualizing on a consistent basis.

Now move into the next phase, which is meditation. Again, flow into this space. Meditate on your vision with words, affirmations, and scriptures that align with it. It could even be one word like YES that welcomes all that you see into your life. I shared earlier with you what my mantra is: My peace, happiness, and success are non-negotiable. Well, often times I will just meditate on those three words, PEACE, HAPPINESS, SUCCESS, repeating them softly to myself as I am picturing my life filled with more of it. I know that my words have power, so I like to say them out loud.

Scriptures from the Bible are powerful because they are reminders that what you are visualizing is possible despite the challenges you might be facing. Scripture gives us hope and helps increase our faith. It also acknowledges God's promises and is a reminder that He wants us to be blessed and prosperous. Write out your favorite affirmations and scriptures on the blank pages and come back to them during this meditation time.

SIDE NOTE: I'm all for affirmations and prayer but faith without works is dead so don't think you can just speak things into existence. You also have to do the work. There is no way around it.

The next phase is journaling. Putting pen to paper and making the vision plain is a powerful practice. You don't have to write out your vision every day, but a few things that you may want to jot down are new ideas, new dreams, new goals and your TO DO list to make it all your reality.

You can also write down negative thoughts, feelings, problems or painful experiences in your journal, as some people find this to be helpful in releasing the pain. I recommend you do this in a separate notebook dedicated to this type of journaling. I remember finding a letter that I wrote to God from a time when I was in an abusive relationship. As I read it, I was thankful that I had moved on from that situation. It brought back so many painful memories that I then had to release the pain again. I was able to do that, no problem. But that time I spent remembering didn't serve me. And at that moment I decided not to keep a record of my pain so the choice is yours. If you enjoy this type of journaling because it is therapeutic, do it. There may come a time when you no longer desire to and that is ok too.

I also like to write down my wins, blessings, breakthroughs, gratitude and anything else that uplifts me. During moments when I may feel down or even ungrateful, I come back to these pages. They serve as a reminder that I am blessed no matter what life looks like.

The final and most important phase is prayer. Prayer is simply a conversation with God. Pray for your family. Pray for your friends. Pray for your relationship. Pray over your job. Pray over your finances. Pray over your health. Pray over your vision. Pray over your goals. Pray over your dreams. Pray for your future. Pray over your life. Ask God to reveal to you your purpose so that you can align your vision with His. Ask God to bless you and enlarge your territory. Ask God to order your steps and to lead the way. Ask God for supernatural clarity, unbreakable confidence and the unshakable courage required to go after your life's vision with excitement and expectation.

You have not because you ask not. So don't be afraid to ask and don't forget to thank him in advance.

Moment of Clarity

What are the top 3 things cluttering your vision right now?

What do you believe about yourself?

What do you believe about your relationships?

What do you believe about your work?

What do you believe about your life?

What do you believe about your future?

In what ways have your beliefs impacted your ability to see yourself being, doing, and having all that you could ever dream of?

Remember, sometimes there is a lie in beLIEf. The things that we have been told or taught isn't all true so check your beliefs and be willing to adopt new ones that properly align with your desires and the word of God.

What actions can you take and are you willing to take NOW to remove all false beliefs that are holding you back from creating the life you want?

How does your future look once all the mental, emotional, spiritual, physical, financial and relationship clutter is removed or released from your life? Be specific and descriptive. Don't overthink this. Just let it flow.

You were created on purpose, with purpose, for a purpose!

Session Eleven Clarify Your Purpose

YOU MUST KNOW WHO YOU ARE AND WHO YOU ARE NOT.

Finding your purpose is a hot topic right now, and many people are seeking out the answer to this question: "WHAT AM I HERE TO DO?" But I want to challenge you to ask yourself this first: "WHO WAS I CREATED TO BE?" When you can answer that question, what you are here to do will come easily. Maybe you already know your purpose, maybe you're still discovering it, or maybe you haven't even considered that you have a purpose. Still, do this work.

The reason why is that most people think they have one grand purpose in life. But that perspective often leaves people uncertain and unhappy with their life. They begin to compare themselves with others who they believe are living their purpose, especially if they are profiting from it. They tend to see themselves as inferior and inadequate. Just know that what God has for you is for you, so don't get caught up in comparison or competition. Discover YOUR purpose and passionately pursue it.

I never really heard people talk about purpose until I started attending church in my early 20's. When I would hear people talk about how they discovered their purpose, I felt left out. I didn't know what my gifts or talents were, let alone why God had created me. As a matter of fact, after all the crap I had been through and had done, I didn't think God thought that much of me anyway. I just knew I was a mom, a teacher and a woman trying my best to be my best. I hated seeing people hurt, so I tried to make them feel better. I hated seeing people struggle, so I tried to help them find solutions. I knew what it was like to be a teen mom and a single mom so I tried to encourage others in the same situation. I loved my high school teacher Ms. Brown, so I wanted to be like her and became a teacher. That's what I knew. But what I didn't know was that all of those things were in alignment with my purpose.

ALL THINGS ARE WORKING FOR YOU GOOD AND HIS GLORY.

God revealed to me years ago that we should stop trying to narrow and water down our purpose to one main reason why He created us. He created me to be a mom and a wife. He also created me to be a teacher and a life coach. I was created to be an author and a light for women living in the dark. God created me to be a daughter, a sister and a friend. He created me for many reasons so I can help Him accomplish many things here on Earth. Every job I hated, every relationship that failed, every challenge I faced, all contributed to discovering and developing my purpose.

So I want to encourage you to relax and stop racking your brain trying to figure out what is that one thing you're supposed to be doing. Instead, live life fully and keep your eyes, ears, and heart open to what God is trying to do through you. There is a purpose to that position you're in right now. There is a purpose to that relationship you're in right now. There is also purpose to that season you're in right now. So, be present and intentional every day and in every way.

When my clients ask for help finding their purpose I ask them the following questions. I want you to answer them and allow this moment of clarity to shed light on who you were created to be and what you were created to do. You may or may not see it right away but keep digging, and it will become clearer and clearer as God pulls back the curtain on your life.

Moment of Clarity

What do you think your life purpose is?

What led you to that idea?

What are your natural gifts and talents?

What are you passionate about?

What are your top interests?

What skills do you already possess?

What are things you do that people often point out?

What would you love to wake up and do every single day even if it was for free?

What is something you've been thinking about doing for a while, and you just can't shake the feeling?

What commonalities do you notice between your gifts, talents, skills, passions and interest?

What is it that you feel you were put on this Earth to do? (It can be multiple things.)

Who do you think you were created to be? Describe who you need to be to fulfill your purpose.

Whatever you come up with is right. It may be for right now, or it could be forever. But that's irrelevant because you're going to focus on being and living versus getting and having. You'll know you're on the right track because it won't feel forced. Not feeling forced doesn't mean easy. It simply means that it feels natural, good and like you are doing what's right for you, what's best for you and what God wants you to do.

If it doesn't scare you dream bigger!

Session Twelve Clarify Your Dreams

NO FEARS. NO DOUBTS. JUST DREAMS.

As children, we were all big dreamers. No fears. No doubts. Just big dreams about who we would be when we grow up, the job we would have, the car we would drive, the house we would live in, the relationships we would enjoy and the life we would live. But then life happens. Hurt, pain, and disappointment show up making our big dreams appear smaller, less attainable and even unrealistic. But now that you've started to release some of that clutter from your past and you're shifting your mindset, you can resume being that crazy dreamer you once were.

I've always dreamed of being a stay at home mom and wife. I wanted the freedom to take my kids to school, pick them up and have hot chocolate chip cookies waiting for them at home. I always wanted to have a husband who I could take lunch and be his lunch, if you know what I mean. I always wanted to live in a neighborhood where I could go for a morning jog before I started my day, without being afraid. Those are just some of the dreams I had. Now, remember, as a single mom of four, being raised in the way I was, these were some pretty sweet dreams that I believed would make me the happiest woman on Earth. I dream much bigger now, but I thank God for that start. Long story short, after 13 years of teaching and six years of running my business as a side hustle, I quit my job to become a full-time life coach. My dream was fulfilled. I get to take my kids to school and pick them up, but the baking cookies only lasted about a month. Ha! Dream fulfilled. I sold my first home that I lived in for ten years and moved to a community where I can enjoy a nice jog. Dream fulfilled. I'm dating someone that I believe will be enjoying my delicious lunches real soon. Dream in the works. I am happy, yes. Will I stop dreaming and striving? Absolutely not. There is so much more I want to be, do and have. This is just the beginning.

NEVER STOP DREAMING.

It really doesn't matter who you are today, how you were raised or what you've done in the past. The possibilities are limitless. You can be more, do better and have the best, but you cannot stop dreaming. Dreaming alone isn't going to make your dreams come true. You do have to take action. You have to move closer to those dreams. The small ones, the big ones, the outlandish ones, all dreams matter. You matter. Your happiness matters. Your life matters. So get out there and create a good one!

Moment of Clarity

WHAT DO YOU REALLY WANT?

If time, money or resources were not an issue, what would you go after? Paint a clear picture of what you want your life to look like. Describe your dream life including EVERYTHING from how you look, feel, speak, act, your finances, people around you, your home, your car, your career, your lifestyle, your relationships, traveling, and anything else you see in your future.

Close your eyes and spend at least 15 minutes visualizing the life you desire. Use your senses to see it, hear it, smell it, taste it, touch it and feel it. Beware of negative thoughts, doubts, and fears that may come up. You may even feel emotional while doing this exercise. Don't worry. Dreaming can sometimes be scary because it feels too good to be true.

NOTHING IS TOO GOOD TO BE TRUE. YOU DESERVE IT!

Write out your dreams making it as clear as you possibly can. Be so clear that if God said to you right now, "Ask, and you shall receive." you wouldn't leave out a thing.

My Dream Life

My Dream Life

My Dream Life

Be a Goal Getter!

Session Thirteen Clarify Your Goals

Life without goals isn't living - it's existing. Having various goals that you are working towards gives you something to look forward to, making life more meaningful. Let's set some goals - both short term and long term - so you can make sure each day you are getting closer to the dream life you desire and deserve. Now hear me and hear me good: Your goals are not the opposite of your problems. I've worked with many clients who set goals based on where they are today and what they are going through. They usually set goals something like this:

Goal: Get out of this toxic relationship so I can be happy.
Goal: Lose 30 pounds so people can stop asking if I'm pregnant.
Goal: Make more money because I am tired of being broke.
Goal: Move, because I hate my neighborhood.
Goal: Find a new job because my boss gets on my nerves.

The list goes on. These are goals based on temporary situations. I'm not saying you shouldn't leave the guy or the job or the neighborhood. I'm just saying that it's not really a goal. It's more of a desire or task to do. The word goal has a few definitions, but the one I love is "desire and determination to achieve success." My favorite synonyms for the word goal are aim, design, intention, purpose, ambition, aspiration, dream and desire.

Ok, the teacher in me just took over.

But I love words and definitions because they create clarity and focus. Now look back at the examples of the goals I shared. Do you get my point? They are not really goals. They are decisions and moves that need to be made. So, if you have some decisions you need to make, make them now and do what you need to do so that you can set some smart goals and start taking action.

PROGRESS IS THE BEST MOTIVATION.

If you lack motivation, it is because you lack results. The more goals you reach consistently, the more motivated you will be to set new goals and take more action on a daily basis. Feeling successful not only motivates you but will increase your confidence and give you the courage to go after bigger and better things. You can reach all your goals and live your dreams; you just have to go for it.

As a life coach, I have my private clients and the women of *Clutter Free Society* set new goals each month, so they are not just going throughout their days aimlessly. If you don't know where you're going, it's going to be harder to get there. Time, money and energy will always be lost when you don't have a plan. These ladies know what they want, what they need to do to get it and they are held accountable to make it happen.

When setting goals, a lot of people focus solely on body, money and career goals. I encourage them to dig deeper, look wider and farther. They set mindset goals, spiritual goals, relationship goals and many other goals that will help them live a more whole, complete and balanced life. Become a goal getter. Keep your eye on the prize and do what it takes to win it!

In Session Nine of the book, I mentioned S.M.A.R.T goals. There are so many words people use for each letter to describe the goal setting process. However, I want to share with you the one definition that I found most helpful.

SPECIFIC- Make sure you are clear on the EXACT result you are looking for.

MEASURABLE- Make sure to monitor your progress so you can stay on track.

ATTAINABLE- Make sure it's something you can realistically achieve within the set time frame.

RELEVANT- Make sure your goals are important and matter to you (hint: know your "why").

TIME BOUND- Make sure you give yourself a deadline and stick to it.

HERE'S AN EXAMPLE OF A RECENT GOAL A CLIENT AND I SET TO HELP HER REACH HER WEIGHT LOSS GOAL.

I will lose 15 pounds within the next 30 days so I can fit into my favorite size six dress for my graduation.

Now although that is an awesome goal, she still needed a plan. Goals without a plan are just dreams. After you set your smart goals, write your plan. Your plan should be detailed and spell out the actions step you will take to accomplish your goal. It should also include the people and resources needed. This plan will help you create your daily TO DO list to keep you focused, on task and in alignment with your goals and dreams.

Here's the plan we came up with together because as her coach I needed to push her a little bit more than she anticipated. Don't be afraid to push yourself.

- Clean out all junk food from the pantry and refrigerator and give to sister with small children.
- Have a protein shake for breakfast Monday through Friday.
- Meal prep five meals (including lean protein, low carb, and green vegetable) for lunch and ten snacks (including protein) for the week.
- Drink five bottles of water a day. Limit one homemade coffee per day.
- Schedule three days of HITT cardio and two days of strength training every week. Put it on your calendar.
- Cook healthy meals for dinner during the weekend (eat healthier and save money).

- Limit one cheat meal per week and within reason (not an entire cheat day).

- Weigh in weekly and take measurements every two weeks.

She now has the clarity needed to go after her goals with confidence. Guess what...you're next!

Moment of Clarity
SO WHAT ARE YOUR GOALS?

This is the process you can use for any and every goal you set for yourself to ensure you know exactly what you're doing, why you're doing it and how you're doing it. The more clarity you have, the fewer excuses you'll make. Take a few minutes to visualize your dream life again, look at your vision board and then dive into your goal setting and action planning so you can start making moves and creating a life you love.

My Goals

My Goals

My Goals

To be clutter free you must be willing to let go!

Session Fourteen Wrap Up

After reflecting on the various areas of your life, relationships, finances, purpose, dreams, and goals, I want you to download what's on your mind and in your heart. A lot has been discussed and a lot has been revealed so take this time to reflect, release and reset. Your journey is just beginning and I am proud of you for getting started.

My Takeaways

My AHA Moments

Note to Self

Questions for Angel

No more wising, waiting and watching!

So whats next?

Congratulations on completing this journey of self-discovery and shifting from clutter to clarity in key areas of your life. There is so much more to uncover, but this was the perfect start to identify what's been stopping you from living your best life and to get clear on what it is going to take to create a life you love. A clutter-free life!

You wrote down action steps you could take throughout this journaling experience. Now it's time to make your move. Get up, get out and get going! Take inspired action and move on those high vibes and new ideas now. I would love to hear about your clutter to clarity experience, get to know more about you and help you take action consistently according to what you have declared necessary to win in all areas of your life.

Also, as your life coach, I want to answer all the questions you have and hold you accountable. This is to ensure that you continue the decluttering process so you can reach all of your goals and get to live your dream life sooner than later. I know that sometimes lacking clarity, confidence or courage makes it hard to do the things you know you need to do but you don't have to do it alone.

I am here to encourage, empower, guide, coach and support you every step of the way. I committed to helping you declutter your life, make powerful decisions, create breakthroughs and become unstoppable.

Ready to get started?

Find out more about how I can help you and how you can become a member of Clutter Free Society at www.helpingotherstransform.com

About the Author

Angel Richards is a mother of 4, life coach, educator and entrepreneur. She is the CEO of *Helping Others Transform*, a lifestyle empowerment company dedicated to helping women de-clutter their lives, create breakthroughs and become unstoppable. She is also the leader of the #clutter-free movement that has women world-wide focused on having unlimited clarity, undeniable confidence and unshakable courage so they can move past their hurts, habits and hang ups in life & love. Angel is the founder of *Clutter Free Society*, an online community that provides classes, coaching and accountability among like-minded women who are committed to doing the work that will help them heal and thrive. Angel has helped thousands of women transform their lives from clutter to clarity and is the author of the transformative self-help book *Clutter to Clarity: De-clutter Your Life, Reach Your Goals, Live Your Dreams*.

**To learn more about Angel Richards
visit www.helpingotherstransform.com**